Chepsto

Chepstow Bulwarks Camp
Runston Church

Rick Turner MA, FSA

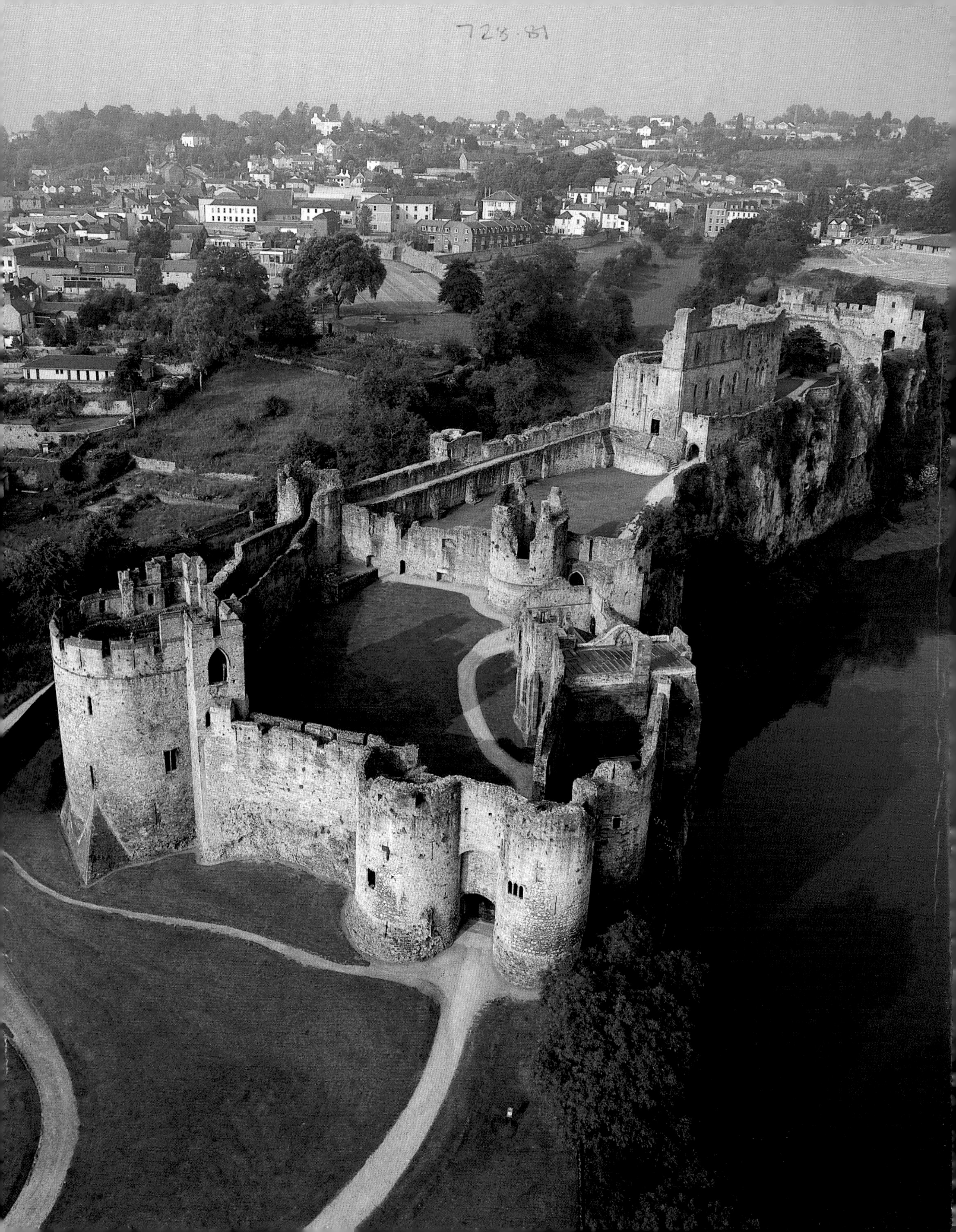

Introduction

'Some fanciful antiquaries have attributed the construction of the castle to Julius Caesar, without considering that he was never in these parts ...'
William Coxe, *An Historical Tour in Monmouthshire, Part II* (London 1801).

Chepstow is a magnificent castle strung out along a lengthy limestone promontory on top of tall cliffs overlooking the river Wye. It is perhaps the best place in Britain to see how the defensive capabilities of castles evolved in response to improvements in the weapons and tactics of potential attackers — a process that can be traced through more than six hundred years from the eleventh to the seventeenth century.

The builders of Chepstow Castle were some of the wealthiest and most powerful men of the medieval and Tudor periods: Earl William fitz Osbern, (d. 1071); King William I (1066–87); William Marshal, earl of Pembroke (d. 1219); Roger Bigod, earl of Norfolk (d. 1306) and Charles Somerset, earl of Worcester (d. 1526). They possessed lands and held political power not only in Wales, but also across England and — in some cases — in Normandy and Ireland too. Chepstow Castle was just one stronghold and residence in a network spreading across their vast and far-flung estates. They were constantly on the move, travelling with a large household, a retinue of knights and soldiers, and a long baggage train. The remarkable suites of accommodation you will find in the castle were just shells into which these great men would bring their gold and silver vessels, rich silk and woollen cloths, and brightly painted furniture. They would entertain their guests, households and tenants on a lavish scale before moving on after a few days or weeks, leaving the castle in the care of its constable, with a small force of soldiers and domestic servants.

Chepstow Castle was also symbolic of the great power of these mighty lords at this gateway into Wales, a place where they would have given audience to their dependent lords and knights, held courts to maintain their rule of law, and demonstrated their courtly and chivalrous grace. When they were elsewhere, this great castle was a permanent reminder of their magnificence: it dominated the medieval town which developed around its foot, the bridge which provided access for travellers into south Wales and the river which was a main highway of the period.

Opposite: Chepstow Castle seen from the north-east, stretching along a narrow limestone promontory high above the river Wye (Skyscan Balloon Photography for Cadw).

Below: The builders of Chepstow Castle were rich and powerful men who would have entertained guests on a lavish scale. In this early fourteenth-century manuscript illustration, a nobleman, his family and guests dine at high table, whilst musicians entertain them (British Library, Additional Ms. 28162, f. 10v).

A History of Chepstow Castle

The Normans at Chepstow

Throughout his life, William the Conqueror, duke of Normandy and king of England, was surrounded and supported by an inner circle of confidants drawn from his kinsfolk and from the leading families of his duchy. According to William of Poitiers, writing in the eleventh century, best loved of these was his oldest companion, William fitz Osbern, son of the young duke's steward, whom he had known since 'they had been boys together'. It may have been fitz Osbern who suggested to William that he should invade England and press his claim to be king. Whatever the precise nature of the events, it was fitz Osbern who persuaded the sceptical Norman barons to support this adventure. It was fitz Osbern, too, who contributed sixty ships filled with his own men to the invasion fleet.

Following the Battle of Hastings (1066), and his coronation as king, William richly rewarded his most loyal supporters. He granted William fitz Osbern the personal title of earl and the lands of the Anglo-Saxon earldom of Hereford, and extensive parts of the adjacent shires, including Chepstow. Writing some fifty years after the events, the monk–chronicler, Orderic Vitalis, recorded that the king set him up 'to fight the bellicose Welsh' and to build castles in 'suitable places'. That fitz Osbern was a most trusted servant is confirmed by his appointment as one of two vice-regents of England, when the king returned to Normandy in 1067. But fitz Osbern was not to enjoy this powerful position for long, for in 1071 he met his death at the Battle of Cassel in Flanders. Described as the 'bravest of the Normans', he was succeeded by his son, Roger de Breteuil, a man of much weaker character and dubious loyalty to the king. In 1075, he plotted with Ralph, earl of Norfolk and Suffolk, to overthrow William and divide England between themselves. However, barons loyal to the memory of William fitz Osbern captured Roger by the river Severn; he was imprisoned by the king and his estates were forfeited to the Crown. Within nine years of the Conqueror's arrival in England, the fitz Osbern family's fortunes had evaporated.

Domesday Book, compiled in 1086, baldly states that 'Earl William built the castle of Estriguil', or Chepstow, and there is no reason to dispute this assertion. Earl William also founded a Benedictine priory within the town that soon developed outside the castle gates. This was a daughter house of the monastery he had founded at Cormeilles (Eure) in Normandy. But Chepstow was just one of a number of fortifications built to secure the border — or March — between England and Wales. Also recorded in *Domesday Book* are a number of other castles either built or refortified by fitz Osbern. Those at Richard's Castle, Wigmore, Clifford and Ewyas Harold in Herefordshire and that at Monmouth secured the southern March, whilst the earl of Shrewsbury, and a little later, the earl of Chester built similar lines of castles to control the central and northern Marches.

The castles developed by the Normans to secure their newly invaded territories were generally of the

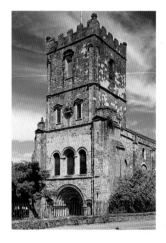

Above: The Benedictine priory at Chepstow, now St Mary's parish church, was founded by William fitz Osbern (d. 1071) as a daughter house of the monastery he had established at Cormeilles (Eure) in Normandy.

Opposite: The great tower, begun in the later eleventh century, is the earliest surviving building at Chepstow and remained the focus of the castle throughout the Middle Ages.

Left: The opening of the Gloucestershire section of Domesday Book *records that 'Earl William built the castle of Estriguil', or Chepstow (The National Archives: PRO, E31/2, f. 162a).*

This scene from the Bayeux Tapestry shows Duke William of Normandy feasting with his half-brother, Bishop Odo of Bayeux, and his barons shortly before the Battle of Hastings. William fitz Osbern, who was one of the duke's closest confidants and one of the principal commanders in the invading army, was probably amongst those at the feast (Musée de la Tapisserie, Bayeux, France. With special authorization of the City of Bayeux/Bridgeman Art Library).

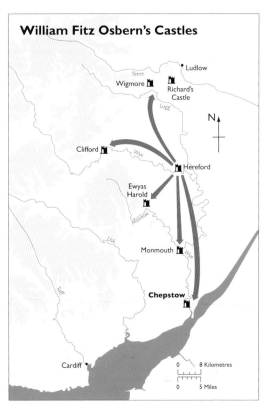

William Fitz Osbern's Castles

Architectural parallels can be drawn between the late tenth-century great tower at Langeais (Indre-et-Loire) and Chepstow's great tower.

motte-and-bailey or ringwork type. Made of earth and timber, they could be erected quickly to provide a stronghold for what were often small garrisons. Richard's Castle, Clifford and Ewyas Harold were of this type; Chepstow, Monmouth and Wigmore, however, were built to take advantage of naturally defended locations. At Chepstow, the river cliffs to the north and the steep valley of the Dell to the south were formidable natural defences. The rock-cut ditch of the upper bailey and the marked change in slope in the middle bailey provided the western and eastern limits of fitz Osbern's castle. This enclosed an area about 340 feet long by up to 65 feet wide (approximately 103m by 20m).

Within this enclosed area is the great tower, which must have dominated the rest of the Norman castle. Built on a grand scale, it measured some 120 feet long by 45 feet wide (36m by 14m), with a formidable windowless façade to the landward or southern side and a line of windows looking north over the river Wye. A band of Roman tiles and some other Roman stonework seem to have been deliberately used in its construction. Inside, there appear to have been just two enormous rooms, one

on each floor. The ground floor comprised a huge basement, or undercroft, which was entered by a doorway in the north wall and lit by three small windows. In contrast, the floor above was approached via an elevated and highly carved doorway on the east side of the tower, which opened into a lobby from where visitors could climb a narrow mural staircase to enter the first-floor room through a door in the south-eastern corner.

An arcade of semicircular-headed niches lined the west and south walls of this chamber and may have extended along the east wall as well; the niche in the centre of the south wall was notably larger. Traces of white and orange plaster survive in the niches on the west wall and the vivid patterns hint at a highly coloured decorative scheme. Lit by seven unglazed semicircular-headed windows in the north wall, the Norman great tower is devoid of any other internal features, except for a doorway alongside the windows, which must have led via an external wooden staircase to the upper part of the Norman castle.

Traditionally, most scholars have assumed that William fitz Osbern built the great tower as part of the castle, which — as *Domesday Book* records — he established at Chepstow. But there are several important reasons for questioning this view. Fitz Osbern held the lands of the earldom of Hereford for only four years, between 1067 and his death in 1071, during which time he was constantly on the move between Normandy and England, campaigning on behalf of King William I. Moreover, the centre of his earldom was Hereford, whereas Chepstow was situated at the south-western tip of his estates on what was potentially a hostile frontier. This combination of circumstances could have made construction of the great tower very difficult.

Nevertheless, if fitz Osbern did build the great tower, it is reasonable to assume that it would have been equipped to provide his main domestic accommodation in the castle. Although it is difficult to identify a typical domestic arrangement of the second half of the eleventh century — because there are so few secular buildings of this date in England and Wales — it is possible to look for parallels in the keeps and towers of Normandy, which survive in greater numbers. These buildings normally contained a large cellar, a hall, a chamber, a latrine, often a chapel and access to a kitchen and other service rooms; they also fulfilled the role of a defensive stronghold at the centre of the castle. In contrast, Chepstow's great tower is equipped with only an undercroft, one vast first-floor room — which has few attributes of the later medieval great hall — and a wall-walk with no evidence for crenellations or arrowloops to protect the castle's defenders. The great tower simply does not seem to possess adequate domestic facilities for a great magnate like Earl William, or for his son, Roger of Breteuil, who held the castle after the death of his father until 1075.

One other clue to the builder of the great tower is the distinctive chip-carved saltire (criss-cross) pattern used on the lintel and tympanum above the east doorway, which can be compared with similar examples from buildings elsewhere. In Normandy, this decoration can be found at Nôtre-Dame-sur-l'Eau, Domfront (Orne), and the church of La Trinité, Caen (Calvados), in the late 1050s and 1060s. Early English examples occur in St John's Chapel, Tower of London and Winchester Cathedral in the late 1070s. However, exactly the same pattern also occurs much later, for example, in the round chapel at Ludlow Castle, which may date from the 1120s. This wide range of dates means that a different patron may have been responsible for Chepstow's great tower.

Left: The principal entrance to the great tower. The lintel and tympanum are decorated with a distinctive chip-carved saltire pattern. Ludlow Castle's round chapel, perhaps built in the 1120s, has similar carving (above).

Below: Although the great tower is the earliest surviving building at Chepstow, there is virtually no evidence for the surrounding enclosure. This artist's impression of the castle suggests one possible form of the late eleventh-century defences and associated domestic buildings (Illustration by Chris Jones-Jenkins, 2002).

The White Tower at the Tower of London, begun by William the Conqueror, contained a great hall, which may have served as an audience chamber. The tower also housed a chapel decorated with an early English example of the chip-carved saltire pattern seen on the great tower at Chepstow (Historic Royal Palaces).

Above: A contemporary image of King William I on a silver penny minted during his reign (National Museum of Wales).

Right: William I is known to have visited Wales only once, in 1081. It is at this time that he may have established the castle on the site of the Roman fort at Cardiff; the impressive mound — or motte — survives beneath the later shell keep.

Roger of Breteuil forfeited his father's estates to the Crown in 1075 and they were to remain in royal hands through the reigns of William I, William II (1087–1100), and — until about 1115 — Henry I (1100–35). King William I certainly seems to have attached great symbolic significance to his role as king of England. During his visits to England, William favoured the existing Anglo-Saxon palaces at Winchester, Westminster and Gloucester, where, according to the *Anglo-Saxon Chronicle*, he held crown-wearing ceremonies 'three times a year' — at Easter, Whitsuntide and Christmas — with 'all the powerful men from all over England'. William also initiated the building of other great towers such as the White Tower at the Tower of London and the palace-keep at Colchester Castle, and they too fulfilled a ceremonial role. Both buildings contained great halls — or audience chambers — furnished with niches, where it is thought that the king sat to receive homage. Such an arrangement recalls the plan of the first-floor room in Chepstow's great tower (pp. 6, 28–29). With its arcade of niches lining the walls, perhaps this room also served as an audience chamber, where Norman lords could do homage to their king or the Welsh princes could pay tribute to their powerful neighbour and overlord. Maybe the deliberate use of bands of Roman tile, some Roman stonework and Roman architectural forms was intended to announce a new royal presence at this gateway into south Wales.

William I is known to have come to Wales only once, in 1081, when he marched through south Wales at the head of a substantial entourage and army, on what was ostensibly a pilgrimage to the shrine of St David. In reality, the visit was probably as much a show of strength and an opportunity to exact tribute from the new leader of south Wales, Rhys ap Tewdwr (d. 1093), with whom the king had reached an agreement to ensure relative peace and stability in the south of the country. It is now generally accepted that William established the castle and mint at Cardiff at this time; perhaps Chepstow's great tower was also begun. William, however, does not appear to have visited Chepstow; nor did his successors, William II and Henry I, who actively encouraged the conquest of south Wales. The great tower may therefore never have been used for the purpose for which it was intended, yet, despite this, it was to remain the focus of the castle for the rest of the Middle Ages.

Chepstow Castle and the Marshal Family

Chepstow Castle remained in royal hands until about 1115, when Henry I granted the lordship to Walter fitz Richard of Clare (d. 1138), whose family held the castle for most of the twelfth century. Although neither Walter nor his successors appear to have undertaken any major work at Chepstow, he was responsible for the foundation of nearby Tintern Abbey in 1131. In 1176, Earl Richard — perhaps better known as Strongbow, the conqueror of the Irish province of Leinster — died, leaving first a son, Gilbert (d. 1185), and then a young daughter, Isabel (d. 1220), as heir to his great estates in Normandy, England, Wales and Ireland. As a minor, Isabel was made a ward of King Henry II (1154–89), and, although she spent some time at Chepstow, the castle was held by the Crown on her behalf and placed in the charge of a royal constable. Isabel was now one of the greatest heiresses in the country and, in 1189, the king promised her in marriage to his faithful knight, William Marshal (about 1147–1219).

William Marshal was one of the most remarkable men of the age, not least because his life story can be followed in a biographical French poem — *Histoire de Guillaume le Mareschal* — written soon after his death. Born the youngest son of an English knight, with little hope of inheriting property or wealth, he travelled to France whilst still in his teens and entered the household of his kinsman, William de Tancarville, chamberlain of Normandy. The Tancarville household provided not only first-class military training, but also some experience of politics and courtly life; William Marshal was knighted when he was twenty. With only his horses and his armour as possessions, Marshal began to make his reputation as a soldier in the wars that rumbled between England and France, and most notably as a successful participant in the tournaments of the day. These were not the jousts of later centuries, but mock battles where magnates fielded teams of knights under the command of professional soldiers like Marshal. The object was to capture and then ransom members of the opposition in no-holds-barred combat.

William Marshal appears to have been a big, handsome, confident man, quick-witted and loyal.

Left: The magnificent tomb effigy of William Marshal (d. 1219) in the Temple Church, City of London. Marshal's colourful life is recorded in a French poem — Histoire de Guillaume le Mareschal *— which traces his rise from a penniless knight to be the powerful and rich earl of Pembroke and marshal of England. In 1189, William Marshal married the heiress of Chepstow, Isabel of Clare, and soon began to modernize the castle.*

Although able and astute, it was William Marshal's reputation for loyalty that allowed him to serve successfully four Plantagenet kings during what were often politically turbulent times. This mid-thirteenth-century manuscript illustration depicts Henry II (1154–89), Richard I (1189–99), John (1199–1216) and Henry III (1216–72) (British Library, Royal Ms. 14 C VII, f. 9).

William Marshal gained renown as a soldier in the wars between England and France and as a successful tournament participant. This fourteenth-century manuscript illustration depicts Richard I (1189–99) in battle at Arques (Seine-Maritime), Normandy (British Library, Royal Ms. 16 G VI, f. 357v).

The great round keep at Pembroke Castle built by William Marshal early in the thirteenth century, after he had been created earl of Pembroke in 1199.

These were qualities that attracted royal patrons: first, Queen Eleanor of England (d. 1202) in 1168, and then, from 1170 until his death in 1183, her eldest son and heir designate to the throne of England, Prince Henry.

Marshal came to act as protector, tutor and companion to the young prince in what were often politically turbulent times. Such was his success that he became powerful enough to raise his own banner — half green, half gold with a red lion rampant — and he had his own company of knights. When Henry was dying in 1183, he charged the faithful William to take his cloak to the Holy Sepulchre in Jerusalem, and on his return from the Holy Land in 1186 he joined the military household of King Henry II. Here, he was kept in constant action defending the king's interests in France, to be rewarded in 1187 with his first substantial grant of land, the royal estate of Cartmel in Lancashire. Two years later, Henry's son, Richard (d. 1199), rebelled against his father; William remained fiercely loyal to the old king, but he spared Richard in a skirmish when he might otherwise have taken his life. In 1189, Richard was crowned king and, in recognition of Marshal's loyalty, honoured his father's wish and gave him in marriage the rich Clare heiress, Isabel. From a poor, but chivalrous knight, William Marshal was transformed into one of the richest and most powerful men in the kingdom.

Marshal was to remain active in politics throughout the reign of Richard I (1189–99),

including a period as one of four co-justiciars left to manage the country when the king went on crusade in 1190. He later supported King John's accession to the throne, in return for which he was created earl of Pembroke in 1199 and gained extensive new lands. And despite the later loss of the king's favour, by 1215 he was acting as John's chief negotiator in the drafting of Magna Carta. Thereafter he remained the king's most important councillor until John's death in the following year. William Marshal then acted as regent of England on behalf of the young King Henry III (1216–72), until his own death, aged over seventy, in 1219.

William Marshal built on a prodigious scale, transforming Usk Castle, and later Pembroke Castle, where he added the great round keep. He was also very active in another Clare inheritance — the province of Leinster, south-east Ireland, where he built the castle and walled town of Kilkenny and established the town of New Ross. Nor did William Marshal neglect matters spiritual: amongst a number of religious foundations, he established the Cistercian abbey of Tintern Parva, County Wexford, as a daughter house of Tintern Abbey, following a vow taken during a storm on the Irish Sea in 1201.

When William Marshal married Isabel of Clare in 1189, he found himself in possession of an old, outmoded castle, which may have been little altered since the late eleventh century. With newly acquired wealth, a leading position in the governance of the English kingdom and a considerable knowledge of the most advanced military techniques gained during his years in France and the Holy Land, he was ideally placed to create a formidable, but comfortably equipped fortress, commensurate with his power and status.

Recent dendrochronological (tree-ring) dating of the castle doors from the main gatehouse suggests that work started with the lower bailey defences in the 1190s, some twenty to thirty years earlier than previously thought. The gatehouse was constructed as a gateway defended by two round towers (p. 49). This was a revolutionary design, which appears to mark the transition from square-towered gatehouses and simple gateways alongside square towers to a form that eventually developed into the massive gatehouses of the late thirteenth century, such as that seen at Harlech, Gwynedd. The defences were continued by building a curtain wall on the east and south sides of the lower bailey, probably with a tower

A reconstruction of the main gatehouse as it may have looked soon after its completion some time in the 1190s. The barbican is cut away to show the defensive arrangement at the entrance to the gate-passage (Illustration by Terry Ball, 2002).

The Castle Doors

Remarkably, a number of wooden doors have survived at Chepstow Castle and these have been dated using dendrochronology, or tree-ring dating. Dendrochronology involves comparing the pattern of growth rings of a sample taken from timber with a dated sequence of tree rings derived from living trees and other samples from the same region. Where samples match the reference sequence, then the calendar date of the last ring on the sample can be given, and the date when the tree was felled and when its timber was used can be estimated.

The doors in the upper and middle bailey gateways at Chepstow are made of two layers of elm and oak boards, clenched together with a regular pattern of iron nails. The outer rings of the planks had been trimmed away when the doors were made, resulting in an estimated date of construction in the first half of the sixteenth century. The three triangular holes cut in each door belong to the Civil War and were for muskets or pistols. The two doors surviving in Marten's Tower are of similar materials and construction, and so are likely to date from the Tudor remodelling of that tower.

The most exciting results came from the doors, which, until 1962, were in the main gatehouse and are now in the exhibition. Samples suggest that these doors were made no later than the 1190s, which has meant that the history of the castle has had to be reviewed. The doors are revolutionary in their construction. The iron plates, which sheathed the outer wooden face to stop attackers from burning or battering the doors down, are held by iron straps and massive nails that are driven through diagonal washers or 'roves' on the back of the door — a contemporary ship-building technique. The wooden lattice framework on the back of the doors is the earliest evidence of developed mortice-and-tenon joints known in Britain. At over 800 years old, these are believed to be the oldest castle doors surviving in Europe and are a testament to the skill of the craftsmen employed by William Marshal.

The rear face of the original castle doors from the main gatehouse, which date from no later than the 1190s.

The tomb effigy of William Marshal the younger (d. 1231) lies close to that of his father in the Temple Church, City of London. William was the first of the five Marshal brothers to hold Chepstow, during which time they modified the great tower and constructed the stone defences of the upper barbican.

Gilbert Marshal (d. 1241) succeeded his brother, Richard, in 1234, but died seven years later from injuries sustained during a tournament at Ware, Hertfordshire. This mid-thirteenth-century manuscript illustration from Matthew Paris's Chronica Majora *shows Gilbert being dragged along by his horse after his fall (The Master and Fellows of Corpus Christi College, Cambridge, Ms. 16, f. 148).*

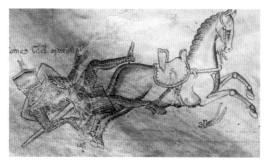

The magnificent great hall at Winchester Castle, built by Henry III. Contemporary work on the great tower at Chepstow was of an equally high quality and may have been influenced by the royal work at Winchester and elsewhere (© Hampshire County Council, 2006).

at the south-east corner. The lower bailey may also have contained additional domestic buildings given that the Norman great tower is unlikely to have provided adequate accommodation for William Marshal and his retinue.

A second line of defence was created between the lower and middle baileys. Two round towers were built — one to the south at the junction with the lower bailey curtain wall, overlooking the Dell, and one alongside a simple, arched gateway close to the riverside cliff. These rounded towers are very early examples of this style of defence in England and Wales, and were linked by a curtain wall with deep embrasures and arrowloops at ground-floor level. The south curtain wall was then extended westwards from the corner tower, via a D-shaped interval tower (built for additional protection), to join the corner of the great tower.

Having completed the defence of the lower and middle baileys, the Norman curtain walls of the upper bailey were replaced with a much taller curtain wall, and a rectangular tower — Marshal's Tower — was built in the south-west corner of the castle. This tower contained a fine first-floor chamber, built over what seems to have been a kitchen. It is in the remotest part of the new castle and probably served as a private retreat for William and his wife. An account of 1271–72 refers to a 'gloriette' (pp. 16, 42) and the *camera comitesse* — countess's chamber — either of which could refer to the main room in this tower. Alongside was another simple, arched gateway and the curtain wall, which extended out to the cliff.

In 1217, the young King Henry III visited the castle. Two years later, in 1219, William Marshal died and was succeeded in turn by each of his five sons who held the family estates until 1245. In 1228, William Marshal II received a gift of ten oaks from the king for works on the tower at Chepstow. This may indicate the beginning of the work which saw the Norman first-floor chamber (p. 6) divided into two by a pair of sumptuously decorated arches, and provided with windows in a refined Early English Gothic style along the north wall. William died in 1231, and was succeeded by his brother, Richard, who quarrelled with Henry III. After what almost amounted to a civil war, Richard withdrew to Ireland, where he was killed in 1234. Before the rift, however, Henry had revisited Chepstow and spent some time at the castle in December 1232.

Richard was succeeded by Gilbert, who was soon reconciled with the king. Royal favour was confirmed with grants of lands in Carmarthen and Cardigan, and the custody of Glamorgan following a period of Welsh resurgence. In 1234, Gilbert was rewarded with a grant of 'fifty good oaks' for joisting the great tower, the west end of which was raised to create additional accommodation. Just four months later Gilbert received the gift of another twenty-five oaks to repair the *jarruyllium* — most commonly translated as the palisade — at the castle. This may refer to the upper barbican — where the defences were later rebuilt in stone, probably also by Gilbert. The later work also included the construction of the south-west tower (pp. 34–35), which was designed to provide a very comprehensive field of fire at this vulnerable corner of the castle, and a simple west gateway.

Gilbert died in 1241, caused by injuries sustained at a tournament held at Ware in Hertfordshire. He was succeeded by his brothers, Walter and Anselm, who both died in 1245.

What the Marshal brothers had achieved at Chepstow was not only the extension of the western defences, but also the transformation of the great tower. This now comprised a withdrawing chamber beyond the arches, and a more private bedchamber on the floor above. The architectural detailing is of the highest quality and follows the contemporary work being undertaken by Henry III at Winchester Castle and Clarendon Palace.

In 1245, however, there were no surviving male heirs. Therefore, the estate was divided amongst the Marshal brothers' five sisters or their descendants, with Chepstow passing to the eldest sister, Maud, who had married Hugh Bigod, third earl of Norfolk (d. 1225). Maud was the mother of Roger Bigod (d. 1270), fourth earl of Norfolk, and when she died in 1248 her son inherited her share of the Marshal inheritance, including the title of Earl Marshal and Chepstow Castle. There is no evidence that Roger undertook any new building at the castle; he did, however, visit and enjoy the hunting on a number of occasions.

By 1245, when the last of the Marshal brothers, Anselm, had died, the defences at Chepstow had reached the extent, if not the form, we see today. This artist's impression of the castle shows domestic buildings in the lower bailey and a round tower at the south-east corner, though we cannot be certain of the arrangements at this time. The form of the south-west tower in the upper bailey and the entrance arrangements for the great tower are also conjectural (Illustration by Chris Jones-Jenkins, 2002; with amendments, 2006).

Above: Chepstow Castle passed to Roger Bigod (d. 1306) in 1270. This impression of his seal shows his coat of arms (The National Archives: PRO, E26/1, seal 78).

Below left: The Bigod arms appear in this illuminated initial from the early fourteenth-century Gorleston Psalter *(British Library, Additional Ms. 49622, f. 70v).*

Below right: King Edward I (1272–1307), with whom Earl Roger sometimes had a difficult relationship, is shown here in a contemporary drawing (The National Archives: PRO, E 368/72).

Roger Bigod's Chepstow Castle

When Roger died in 1270, his nephew, another Roger Bigod (about 1245–1306), became fifth earl of Norfolk. Not only did he inherit Chepstow Castle and vast estates across southern England, south Wales and south-east Ireland from his uncle, but also the post of Earl Marshal. Roger was to hold the earldom of Norfolk for more than thirty years between 1270 and his death in 1306, a period that was almost contemporary with the reign of King Edward I (1272–1307). Almost inevitably, the lives of the king and one of his greatest magnates were closely entwined, and their relationship was at times stormy.

Initially, however, Earl Roger was a loyal servant of the king — able and willing to raise a force of soldiers for the royal army at his own expense. He supported the king in the Welsh wars of 1276–77 and 1282–83, during which Edward fought Llywelyn ap Gruffudd of Gwynedd (d. 1282) and eventually subdued Wales. He also intervened as peacemaker on the king's behalf in Ireland in 1280, helped put down a Welsh uprising in south Wales in 1287 and, later, he was to lead the king's armies in Scotland. During this period, Earl Roger is thought to have enclosed Chepstow within a stone town wall

(p. 51–52) in order to control access to the town and the payment of tolls and taxes.

Earl Roger's inherited lands and title were to bring him great wealth — perhaps as much as £4,000 a year — but he also inherited considerable debts to the Crown from his father and uncle. These debts and the constant and disproportionate demands for tax to pay for the wars in Wales, France and later Scotland were to lead to an open dispute with the king. Another source of growing tension between the earl of Norfolk and the king was Edward's usurpation of his rights as Earl Marshal.

Pressure mounted during the years 1293 to 1296, until, in 1297, the barons were faced with the king's demand for an invasion of France and an expedition against Flanders. At a parliament in Salisbury, Earl Roger refused an order to lead an army to Gascony, instead of serving as Earl Marshal alongside the king in Flanders. A chronicler, Walter of Guisborough, recorded that the king burst out 'By God, Sir Earl, either go or hang', to which the earl replied, 'By the same oath, O king, I will neither go nor hang'.

Following this parliament the earl of Norfolk and Humphrey de Bohun, earl of Hereford (d. 1298), were said to have raised a force of 1,500 cavalry and a multitude of foot soldiers, and they refused to join the king's muster. On 22 August, they marched into the Exchequer and forbade officials to raise the tax for the war. In partnership with the City of London, they sought confirmation of Magna Carta and the

Forest Charter, and demanded the inclusion of new clauses that would oblige the king to obtain the consent of his subjects before levying a new tax. The king's hand was forced by the success of William Wallace (d. 1305) at the Battle of Stirling Bridge in Scotland, and he agreed to the earls' demands to ensure their loyalty in the Scottish campaign of 1298.

Having achieved his objective, Roger Bigod's power seems to have collapsed. His greatest ally, Humphrey de Bohun, died in 1298, and, according to Walter of Guisborough, he was in financial difficulty, having spent a large amount of money raising an army against the king. In 1302, Roger Bigod temporarily relinquished his titles and lands to King Edward. When he regained them, just weeks later, Edward granted him an extra £1,000 of lands, rents and farms on the understanding that should he die without direct heirs, the Bigod estate would revert to the Crown. In 1305 Edward pardoned his debts and when Roger died childless in 1306, his estates — including the lordship and castle of Chepstow — were returned into royal hands.

Roger Bigod's life was typical of many great magnates of the day. He had a huge income from his estates, particularly from the sale of wool in the markets of Flanders. He controlled a large household, including up to forty knights, that would have moved with him from castle to castle, and could raise and equip a substantial force of soldiers. Earl Roger built on a lavish scale at Chepstow Castle, and erected a hunting lodge at Cas Troggy in the Wentwood, Monmouthshire; he also upgraded the accommodation at Framlingham Castle and restored and extended Bungay Castle, both in Suffolk. He developed sumptuous manor houses at Walton, Suffolk, and Hamstead Marshall, Berkshire, and had a town house in Denburgh Lane, London. In addition, he was a principal patron of the great new Gothic abbey church at Tintern, and made generous donations to other religious orders, including the Black Friars at Gloucester.

Roger Bigod seems to have made Chepstow his main residence and continued to develop William Marshal's fortress into a palatial stronghold. A collection of building accounts from different years within the period 1271–1304 provides a remarkable insight into the sequence of construction, the names and functions of the rooms, the master craftsmen involved and the costs. The earliest reference records

Left: Framlingham Castle, Suffolk, was just one of the many properties owned and improved by Roger Bigod (English Heritage).

Below: The east end of the abbey church at Tintern. Roger Bigod made a series of generous grants to the monks at Tintern, and was remembered by later generations as the 'Founder'.

Above: Roger Bigod undertook the last major phase of building work at Chepstow, equipping the Marshal stronghold with lavish suites of accommodation suitable for a man of his rank and aspirations. This view of the north face of the castle shows the large domestic range that he created in the lower bailey, and the great tower where he extended the top floor.

repairs to an existing building, the gloriette (pp. 12, 42), and general repairs to other parts of the castle. Earl Roger's first objective was to create a new and grand suite of private apartments on the cliff side of the lower bailey. The ingenious design was by the master mason, Ralph Gogun of London (d. 1293), who made full use of the changes in level across the site and provided access to the castle from boats on the river.

The building accounts are missing for the period between 1272 and 1282, during which the hall, cellar, service rooms and earl's chamber were built and work on the kitchen and its associated chambers begun. This new range of buildings was also wholly or partly referred to as the 'Gloriette' and must have been operational when King Edward I and Queen Eleanor and their entourage stayed at the castle for four days in December 1284. Following this visit, Roger Bigod and Master Ralph began work on the 'New (Marten's) Tower', which was not completed until about 1293. This contained a pair of lavish apartments and a small, but exquisitely decorated, chapel. The tower could be isolated from the rest of the castle by portcullises and barred doors. It provided a self-contained lodging for Roger's most distinguished guests, built in the hope, perhaps, of entertaining the king again, a hope to be dashed by his opposition to Edward in 1297.

Having completed the work in the lower bailey, Bigod turned his attention to what must have remained the symbolic and administrative heart of the castle and lordship of Chepstow, the great tower. He extended the upper storey and added corner towers to the eastern end of the tower — giving it a massive presence — roofed the whole tower in lead and built the gallery alongside. As a final embellishment, and perhaps even as an act of defiance, in 1298–99 he commissioned master Reginald the Engineer to make four 'springalds' (giant crossbows) and paid Philip Daniel, carpenter, to construct a great crane to winch them up and mount them on the wall tops of the tower.

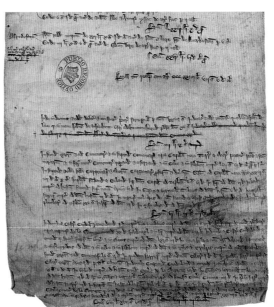

Left: A section of the 1292–93 building accounts for Chepstow Castle, which record expenditure on the building of Marten's Tower and repairs to 'the earl's chamber La Gloriette' (The National Archives: PRO, SC 6/922/25).

Below: An artist's reconstruction of how Roger Bigod's Chepstow Castle may have looked by about 1306 (Illustration by Chris Jones-Jenkins, 2002; with amendments, 2006).

In 1324 Chepstow was granted to Hugh Despenser the younger (d. 1326), the unscrupulous favourite of King Edward II (1307–27). Despenser is seen depicted in a stained glass panel in the choir clerestory at Tewkesbury Abbey (Vicar and Churchwardens, Tewkesbury Abbey).

Right: A nineteenth-century portrait of Sir Charles Somerset, first earl of Worcester (d. 1526), after an unknown artist. His fortunes rose with those of the Tudor dynasty, to which he was related, and he held important offices in the royal household under both Henry VII and Henry VIII. His marriage to Elizabeth Herbert, the heir of William Herbert, earl of Huntingdon, in 1492 brought Charles Somerset extensive estates in south Wales, and in 1504 he was created Baron Herbert. Three years later, Chepstow passed into his hands on the death of Sir Walter Herbert, his wife's uncle (National Portrait Gallery, London).

The Later Middle Ages

Roger Bigod's lands duly passed to Edward I when he died, but the king outlived him by only seven months and so the estates were soon inherited by the new king. Edward II (1307–27) took a considerable interest in the castle, and in 1312 he vested his half-brother, Thomas of Brotherton (d. 1338), with the lordship of Chepstow. There is a sheaf of documents describing a continuing and expensive campaign of repairs — following the stripping of building materials after Bigod's death — and garrisoning and provisioning the castle with up to twelve knights and sixty footmen. The springalds were made good and the armoury was regularly replenished during the constableship of the king's unscrupulous favourite, Hugh Despenser the younger (d. 1326), who was later granted the castle and all its lands in 1324. In October 1326, Edward and Hugh Despenser fled to Chepstow Castle — which they had provisioned, perhaps in expectation of a long siege — rather than face the rebel forces of the king's estranged queen, Isabel (d. 1358), and her companion, Roger Mortimer (d. 1330). They tried to escape by sea to Ireland but were forced to land at Cardiff from where they began a desperate search for refuge. Eventually they were captured; Despenser was executed and the king later met a brutal death in Berkeley Castle, Gloucestershire.

At the end of the fourteenth century, Chepstow Castle passed to Thomas Mowbray, earl of Norfolk (d. 1405). In 1403, he was ordered to garrison and provision the castle against the arrival of Owain Glyn Dŵr (d. about 1415), but the Welsh leader's advance was stopped at Usk and the castle saw no action. During the Wars of the Roses (1455–85), Chepstow was again to provide refuge to fallen royal favourites — Richard Woodville, earl Rivers, and his son, Sir John Woodville — after the Yorkist defeat at the Battle of Edgcote in 1469. Their rival, Warwick 'the Kingmaker' (d. 1471), pursued them to Chepstow where the garrison surrendered the unpopular Woodvilles without a fight. They were taken to Kenilworth Castle and executed.

Tudor Chepstow

Charles, first earl of Worcester (d. 1526), was a cousin of both Henry Tudor, later Henry VII (1485–1509), and Henry's mother, Lady Margaret

Beaufort (d. 1509). He spent his childhood in exile but returned with Henry Tudor when he landed at Milford Haven in 1485. Following their success at the Battle of Bosworth, Charles's career prospered under the new king: in 1496 he became a Knight of the Garter and held a succession of offices in the king's household.

In 1492, Charles married Elizabeth Herbert (d.1507), a ward of Henry VII and sole heir of William Herbert, earl of Huntingdon (d. 1491). This brought him the lordships of Gower, Kilvey, Crickhowell, Tretower and Raglan. In the first decade of the sixteenth century, he acquired other lordships from the king, and in 1507, on the death of Sir Walter Herbert — his wife's uncle — he became lord of Chepstow as well. Created Baron Herbert in 1504, he was now the most powerful man in south Wales.

He remained influential on the accession of Henry VIII (1509–47), who made him lord chamberlain — the head of the royal household. He also undertook a number of military expeditions and diplomatic visits to France and in reward was created earl of Worcester in 1514. However his finest hour came

when he was put in charge of the negotiations for a truce between England and France. This culminated in the remarkable meeting between Henry VIII and the king of France, Francis I (1515–47), with their vast entourages at the Field of the Cloth of Gold, held outside Calais in June 1520. Charles stage managed the construction of a temporary palace within a small town of ornate tents and erected a tiltyard for a great joust. On his death, he was buried in the Beaufort Chantry in St George's Chapel, Windsor, a just reward for his service to the two first Tudor monarchs.

It was Charles, earl of Worcester, who made the first substantial changes to Chepstow Castle since Roger Bigod over 200 years earlier. He transformed the lower bailey into a great court by modifying all the buildings that surrounded it. The most significant change was the relocation of his private apartments from over the service end of the hall to a complex of buildings contrived on either side of the middle bailey curtain wall and within its two towers.

In this arrangement, the earl and his inner circle would have left the high table through the small dais chamber overlooking the river and climbed the stairs to a small but well-lit chamber above. They would

Above: Charles Somerset played an important role in the stage management of the meeting between Henry VIII and the French king, Francis I, at the Field of the Cloth of Gold, outside Calais, in June 1520. This contemporary painting by an unknown artist shows the splendid temporary palace and town of tents erected as the setting for the negotiations (The Royal Collection © 2006, Her Majesty Queen Elizabeth II).

Left: Henry VIII rewarded Charles Somerset for his loyal service to the Crown by creating him first earl of Worcester in 1514, and on his death in 1526 he was accorded the honour of burial in the Beaufort Chantry in St George's Chapel, Windsor. The fine alabaster effigies of the earl and his wife are surrounded by an elaborate gilded iron screen made by Jan van den Einde of Malines, Belgium.

Above: An imaginative reconstruction of how Chepstow Castle may have looked after the changes made to the castle by Charles Somerset in the early sixteenth century. Note the buildings constructed on either side of the middle bailey curtain wall (Illustration by Chris Jones-Jenkins, 2006).

Right: The square-headed windows inserted in the rear face of Marten's Tower are characteristic of the Tudor remodelling of the castle.

then have walked across the top of the middle bailey gateway into rooms within the tower. Beyond the tower, new buildings were added to the front and rear of the curtain wall, which was remodelled to take new fireplaces and doorways. The great chamber and privy chamber may have overlooked the lower bailey and perhaps a gallery was built looking towards the great tower.

Elsewhere in the castle, new windows and fireplaces were introduced into Marten's Tower, the great gatehouse and the chambers overlooking the cliff. The kitchen was fitted with a new fireplace and oven and the surviving doors in the middle and upper bailey gateways seem to date from this period.

Chepstow Castle was by no means the most important of the earl's residences: Raglan Castle was larger and much more magnificent. Nevertheless, the modifications at Chepstow were significant and ingenious, designed to receive the smaller household of a Tudor magnate, who would have demanded more privacy, comfort and light, compared with their medieval predecessors.

The Civil War

At the outbreak of the Civil War in 1642, Henry, fifth earl and later first marquess of Worcester (d. 1646), a Roman Catholic, declared for King Charles I (1625–49). Chepstow was a strategic location at the entrance to south Wales; it controlled the Severn estuary and its links to the important royalist stronghold in Bristol. In April 1643, the parliamentarian general, Sir William Waller (d. 1668), advanced into Monmouthshire but did not take Chepstow Castle and was forced to withdraw.

It was not until October 1645, after the fall of Bristol, when the king's cause was becoming hopeless, that the parliamentarians were able to muster enough heavy artillery to force the surrender of the castle. Sir Thomas Morgan with a force of over 900 men set up a battery of three guns on the hill overlooking the castle. After three days of concentrated fire, a breach was made and the governor, Edmond Fitzmorris, and his 110 men were forced to surrender. Perhaps as important as the capture of the castle were the eighteen cannon, barrels of gunpowder and huge store of provisions it contained.

Left: The parliamentarian commander, Sir Thomas Morgan, besieged Chepstow Castle with a force of over 900 men with three cannon in October 1645. After a bombardment of three days, the the royalist garrison surrendered (Ashmolean Museum, University of Oxford).

Below: During both of the Civil War sieges of Chepstow Castle, the parliamentarian forces breached the defences by positioning their guns on the high ground across the Dell and concentrating their fire on the curtain wall to the west of Marten's Tower.

Right: In 1648, Chepstow was seized by the local royalist, Sir Nicholas Kemeys. In the autumn of that year, besieging parliamentary forces subjected the castle to a fierce artillery barrage. When the defenders surrendered, Kemeys was peremptorily shot (Trustees of The Pennington Mellor Munthe Trust).

In 1648, after the defeat and capture of Charles I, diehard royalists led a number of uprisings, resulting in the second phase of the Civil War. Oliver Cromwell, on route to reduce Pembroke, attacked the town of Chepstow whose walls were lined with royalist musketeers. Colonel Pride's regiment forced the town gate, and the castle governor, Sir Nicholas Kemeys, retreated into the castle with 150 men. Cromwell demanded its surrender. When this was refused, he left Colonel Ewer, with his regiment and four cannon, to reduce it. They razed the battlements, destroyed the garrison's guns and bombarded the interior with mortar shells. They then 'played…with our great guns very hot', and made a breach on the south side 'so low that a man might walk into it'. As Ewer's men prepared to storm the castle, the garrison surrendered and Kemeys was peremptorily shot.

After the war, the lands of the marquess of Worcester were declared forfeit and Chepstow Castle was granted to Cromwell. In 1650, parliament spent £300 on repairs to the castle, which was converted into a military barracks and became a prison for political dissidents.

Right: An engraving from Agostino Ramelli's Le diverse et artificiose machine *(Paris 1588) depicting a stronghold under siege. Similar cannon would have been used during the siege of Chepstow in October 1648 (Science Museum/Science & Society Picture Library)*

Far right: At the end of the Civil War, Chepstow Castle was granted to Oliver Cromwell (d. 1658) and it became a military barracks and prison for dissidents. This painting of Cromwell, by Robert Walker (1599–1658), dates from about 1649 (National Portrait Gallery, London).

Chepstow Castle after the Restoration

Upon the restoration of King Charles II (1660–85) to the throne in 1660, the lordship and town of Chepstow were returned to the marquess of Worcester. The king, however, retained the castle as a fort and barracks, and the marquess's eldest son, Henry, Lord Herbert (d. 1700), was appointed governor. He was charged with raising a company of 100 men and keeping the fortification in good repair.

In 1662, Henry spent £500 on the repair of the castle of Chepstow and he must have continued the work started by Cromwell to adapt the masonry medieval castle into an artillery fortress. The south-west tower and the D-shaped tower in the middle bailey were filled with earth, and platforms were built on the middle bailey corner tower and the main gatehouse to support cannon. The south curtain wall in the upper and middle baileys was lowered and thickened, and that in the lower bailey was rebuilt with a carefully crafted inner wall and an impressive gunport. These walls were topped with lines of musketloops.

Henry succeeded to his father's titles in 1667 but did not live at Chepstow. He built Castle House in Monmouth and, nearby, Troy House, but his main residence was Badminton House, a Palladian mansion in Gloucestershire. He is reported to have maintained a 'princely way of living … ' more lavish than any other except crowned heads'.

In addition to being a barracks, Chepstow Castle acted as a prison for a number of those thought to be a threat to the king. In 1661, Colonel Robert Overton (d. 1678/79) — a parliamentary commander and prominent politician during the Commonwealth — was brought here though he was free again by 1663 when he was re-arrested and taken to Jersey. The most celebrated prisoner was Henry Marten (d. 1680) — a high-living rake and republican politician. Marten was one of fifty-nine people to sign King Charles I's death warrant. He was fortunate that on the restoration of Charles II he escaped execution, unlike so many of his fellow regicides, but was sentenced to life imprisonment. After time spent at Lindisfarne Castle, the Tower of London and Windsor Castle he was moved to what became known as

Above: An artist's impression of the gunport in the south curtain wall, which was created during the rebuilding of the 1660s (Illustration by Chris Jones-Jenkins, 2006).

Left: Henry Somerset, third marquess of Worcester, succeeded to Chepstow on his father's death in 1667. However, he did not live at the castle, preferring other, more modern, residences, such as Castle House, Monmouth.

Following the Restoration, Henry Marten (d. 1680) — republican and regicide — was sentenced to life imprisonment, twelve years of which he served at Chepstow in the tower that now bears his name (National Portrait Gallery, London).

In 1913, Chepstow Castle was used as the setting for the film Ivanhoe, *starring the American actor, King Baggot. Many Chepstow residents were used as extras. Here, a Mr Cartwright is dressed in flamboyant costume as a 'Saracen' (Chepstow Museum).*

Marten's Tower at Chepstow Castle in 1668. He occupied the first-floor room with his long-time mistress, Mary, and his servants the room above. Marten's imprisonment was not too harsh: he was allowed to receive guests and even made calls on the local gentry. He is buried in Chepstow parish church.

We know most about Chepstow Castle during this period from two inventories produced in 1672 and 1679. The latter is the more comprehensive, systematically describing the guns, weapons, munitions and other equipment stored in and around the castle.

It is possible to identify most of the locations described in the inventory in the castle today. The gunports on many of the towers and in the lower bailey south curtain wall would have housed iron and brass guns on wooden carriages. Hundreds of muskets and quantities of ammunition were stored in the rooms of the castle. However the inventory implies that the guns and their carriages were much decayed. Many of the other armaments are old-fashioned and broken. The impression given is more like a military museum rather than a fort and barracks in a state of readiness.

The end of the castle as a fortress and a house was close. In the 1680s, the duchess of Beaufort wrote to her husband saying 'I doe most humbly beseech you never to think more of building at Chepstow'. And that she would 'rather pull down this that was there, than add a stone to it'. She much preferred her new mansion at Badminton, Gloucestershire. The garrison was finally disbanded in 1685 and parts of the castle, including the upper parts of the great tower and most of the internal floors and fittings, were demolished and removed.

Chepstow Castle in Modern Times

During the eighteenth century, much of the lower bailey was converted into an industrial estate. The tower by the middle bailey gateway became a nail manufactory and in the 1760s a glass-blowers' retort was built in the hall to make wine bottles for a Bristol merchant. Large ranges of timber-framed buildings, including a malting kiln, stable and dog kennel, were also erected.

In the last quarter of the eighteenth century, the castle received an increasing number of visitors taking the tour down the river Wye from Ross via Monmouth and Tintern Abbey to Chepstow. The Williams family acted as custodians and lived in parts of the Bigod range in the lower bailey, and they could be summoned by a bell at the main gate. Marten's Tower was still roofed and floored at this time, but contemporary accounts suggest that some visitors were more interested in the shapely ankles of Miss Williams as she climbed the spiral stairs, than in the architecture. The rest of the castle was completely overgrown, penetrated by only the most intrepid visitors.

During the nineteenth century, the industrial works were removed and the eighth duke of Beaufort (d. 1899) cleared out the interior of the castle, laid out paths, erected rustic seats and planted trees, including a massive walnut tree that almost filled the lower bailey by the time it was felled in 1960.

Conservation of the fabric was begun in the late nineteenth century by the Beaufort Estate, and was continued later by the Lysaght family, who acquired the castle in 1905, using the local architect, Eric Francis. Local interest in the castle grew as it became the scene for annual medieval pageants and in 1913 it featured alongside the American actor, King Baggot, in the film, *Ivanhoe*. In 1953, Mr D. R. Lysaght put the castle into the guardianship of the State. Both the castle and the Port, or town, Wall are now maintained by Cadw, the historic environment division of the Welsh Assembly Government.

By the end of the eighteenth century, the castle had become a destination for visitors, including J. M. W. Turner (1775–1851) who visited Chepstow in 1792. In this watercolour painted in 1793, Turner shows Marten's Tower still roofed and the early timber-decked road bridge in the foreground (The Samuel Courtauld Trust, Courtauld Institute of Art Gallery, London).

A Tour of Chepstow Castle

The tour suggests one route around the interior of the castle, which explains how the site was developed and used. It is not intended to be rigid and visitors may investigate the various parts of the castle in any order using the bird's-eye view (inside front cover) or the ground plan (inside back cover) as a guide. Our route, however, begins in the middle bailey, in front of the great tower — the oldest building in the castle.

The Great Tower

This massive rectangular tower, almost 120 feet long by 45 feet wide (36m by 14m), dominates the centre of the castle and is the earliest building remaining on the site. The east elevation is raised on a substantial stone plinth, built on a terrace cut into the limestone bedrock. For a long time the great tower was thought to have been a great hall begun by William fitz Osbern as part of the castle of Estriguil identified in *Domesday Book*. As such, it would be the oldest surviving domestic building in Britain, but its architecture and form suggest that it may date from later in the eleventh century and was perhaps built under the patronage of William the Conqueror (pp. 6–8).

The great tower contains some reused building materials, probably brought from the ruins of the Roman town of *Venta Silurum* — modern-day Caerwent — just over 4 miles (7km) away. Most obvious is the horizontal band of orange Roman tiles, which rises to frame the top of the doorway, but the large blocks of yellow sandstone may also have come from an important Roman building. The elevation was divided by pilaster buttresses, which rose to a projecting stone band and a solid parapet at battlement level. Of the four windows visible, only one of the two small slits, which light a mural staircase, is original; the remaining lancet

windows and the whole of the top storey belong to later alterations.

Entrance was by way of a large rectangular doorway. The semicircular panel, or tympanum, above the doorway is made up of diamond-shaped stones, bedded in an orange mortar made of crushed Roman tile. The tympanum, the two arches above it and the lintel are all chip-carved with saltire (criss-cross) patterns. Access to this doorway was presumably via an external staircase and timber forebuilding, linked to a causeway running up to the north side of the great tower. The rubble stonework would have been covered by white render or limewash and the building capped with a low gabled roof.

Today, the great tower is entered at basement level via a Norman doorway from the late thirteenth-century gallery, which runs alongside, overlooking the river Wye. The basement or undercroft was a vast storeroom. Early fourteenth-century records indicate

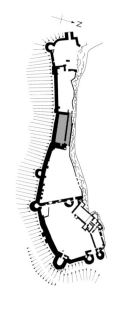

Left: Chepstow's great tower still dominates the castle today. Raised on a massive plinth using a variety of building materials — probably towards the end of the eleventh century — the horizontal band of reused Roman tile is clearly visible on the east elevation.

Opposite: In the foreground of this aerial view of Chepstow Castle is William Marshal's main gatehouse, built in the 1190s to a revolutionary design; to the left is Marten's Tower, built by Roger Bigod at the end of the thirteenth century, and beyond — at the very heart of the castle — is the great tower (Skyscan Balloon Photography for Cadw).

Above: The interior of the great hall, which originally comprised a basement or undercroft with a single large room above. Part of the Norman arcade of niches is visible at the far (west) end. New windows and a second floor were later added, in part by the sons of William Marshal and completed by Roger Bigod, fifth earl of Norfolk.

Right: The fragmentary remains of the eleventh-century wall painting in one of the niches at the west end of the great tower.

that it was used to store the arms and armour held in the castle, and it may also have served as the castle's granary, as the same documents record a handmill for grinding corn here. Lit by three round-headed windows looking over the river, access was via the door from the gallery or from the rear of the main entrance. The floor was formed from the limestone rock surface and the ceiling was made of vast timber joists whose sockets line the long walls. The joists were supported by a long beam, which ran down the centre of the room and fitted into the central sockets in the end walls. This beam would have been carried on massive timber posts. Above the ceiling of wooden planks, there may have been a layer of bedding sand and a stone-flagged floor for the main room above, on which a great central fire could have been safely lit.

The form of the original main room at first-floor level needs to be unravelled from the later phases. Access was via the main doorway at the east end, then up a narrow staircase, within the thickness of the wall, to a plain doorway in the south-east corner. At the opposite (west) end of the room is an arcade of four round-arched stone recesses, or niches. These contain fragments of their original eleventh-century decoration — the oldest surviving secular decoration in Britain. This is best seen in the bay second from left (south), where the recess was filled with a pure white plaster into which was set a band of pink/orange plaster made with crushed Roman tile. This band was overlain by strips of white plaster in a criss-cross pattern and echoes the decoration above the main door. This plasterwork, which seems clumsily applied, has been carefully reproduced in the westernmost recess on the south wall. The two circular windows let light through the west gable.

The arcade of niches continued along the south wall and numbered nine in total, though four were blocked by later masonry. It is clear that the central arch in the south wall was larger. To the left of this arch, close to the right jamb of the window, is a reused Romano-British carving, now thought to represent Venus and her nymphs. The east wall has been modified and may have had a window or two niches. In contrast, the north wall contained seven round-headed windows; one to the east is still open but some of the others can be identified by the distinctive yellow stone that formed their jambs. In addition, there is a round-headed doorway, seemingly

stepping out to nowhere, but which was presumably reached by an external timber stairway. There is no evidence for the subdivision of this great room, nor for any fireplaces or access to any latrines. And, except for the door in the north wall, there is no apparent access to any service rooms or private chambers. The absence of these features together with the plan of the room and its pattern of niches suggests that this building did not serve — as might be expected — as a hall, chamber and chapel, where the lord and his household would have lived, slept and worshipped. Nor was the great tower particularly well equipped militarily, for although the walls were massive and the landward elevations windowless, the main entrance was poorly protected and there were no arrowloops for defenders to use.

It is impossible to be certain how the main chamber was used, but a ceremonial or judicial function seems likely; perhaps the king or his representative sat in the largest niche in the south wall, with other great lords occupying the remaining niches (p. 8). King William I is known to have built new halls elsewhere, for example at Winchester and probably at Gloucester, which were already favoured locations for ceremonial state occasions. Although nothing is known of these buildings, they may have resembled the arcaded great hall illustrated in the Bayeux Tapestry, which is thought to represent William's hall at his palace in Rouen, Normandy. Certainly, something of the magnificence of these buildings is hinted at in the *Prospice*, the blessing prayer used at William's coronation: 'Grant that the glorious dignity of the royal hall may rise before the eyes of all with the greatest splendour of kingly power and that it may seem to glow with

An artist's impression of the great tower at the end of the eleventh century. The vast single first-floor room may have been an audience chamber (Illustration by Terry Ball, 2002; with amendments 2006).

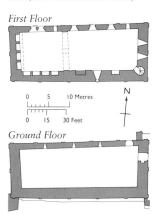

First Floor

0   5   10 Metres

0   15   30 Feet

N

Ground Floor

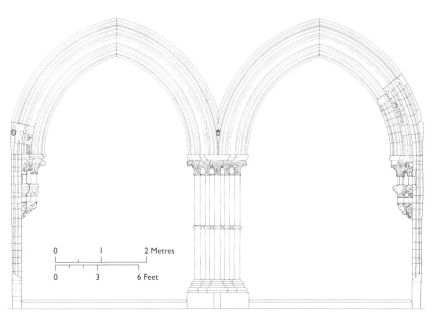

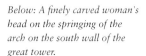

Above: A reconstruction drawing of the two arches that were erected during the transformation of the interior of the great tower by the sons of William Marshal. The arches divided the first floor of the tower into a hall and a smaller chamber. The springing of the arch on the north wall (right), though much damaged, shows that the mid-thirteenth-century alterations were of the highest quality.

Below: A finely carved woman's head on the springing of the arch on the south wall of the great tower.

the brightest rays and to glitter as if suffused by illumination of the utmost brilliance.'

The main first-floor chamber remained unaltered until the second quarter of the thirteenth century when the sons of William Marshal transformed the interior (pp. 12–13). Simple lancet windows were added to the east and south walls; three very handsome mullioned and transomed windows were inserted into the centre of the north wall. Each window had two trefoil-headed lights below quatrefoil tracery, with carved projections to the rear of each mullion and sockets to take the bolts of shutters; only the upper half of each window was glazed. The reveals were equipped with seats and elegant rear arches, which still retain carved stiff-leaf capitals to now-missing columns.

Towards the western end of the room, beyond the three fine north-facing windows, are the remains of a pair of sumptuously decorated arches, which divided the main room into two unequal parts. This was a remarkable structure to have inserted within the Norman great tower, and it has mouldings and carved decoration of the very highest quality. The arches were supported by carved corbels on each side of the tower and a central pier that rose through the floor from the basement below. One corbel took the form of a draped head and the other a squatting man, his bare feet clearly visible. The corbels carry short engaged limestone columns with stiff-leaf capitals. There is a second tier of columns of Purbeck marble, where the stiff-leaf decoration is taken into the body of the wall. The arches consisted of three orders of dressed stone, the middle one of which was decorated with pyramidal foliage bosses.

Beyond the remains of the arches is an even larger and more elaborately decorated window than elsewhere, giving a magnificent view up the gorge of the river Wye. Two windows above this, however, and the great blind arch against the west wall indicate that the Marshal family raised this end of the building by another storey, perhaps as a change of plan during construction. To the right of the two windows is an external doorway, which must have been linked by an external staircase to the one below; and to the right of this doorway is the jamb of another door, which led out onto the parapet walkway.

This sumptuous remodelling of the great tower was in the Early English style, which had been adopted, for example, by King Henry III for his great

hall at Winchester, and by Bishops Joscelin (1206–42) of Wells and Richard Poore (1217–28) of Salisbury for their palaces. It created a more conventional great hall with the lord's table in front of the arches at the west end, furthest from the main door, a private chamber beyond and a bedchamber above. The large central niche in the south wall seems to have been converted into a fireplace and the floor level reduced to the wooden boards on top of the massive joists. Food and drink would have been brought from outside by way of the door in the north wall.

The great tower underwent a final remodelling by Roger Bigod, between 1293 and 1300 (p. 17). The eastern part of the tower was raised to the same height as that of the Marshals' chamber to the west, with corner turrets rising even higher on the east

elevation, and a floor was inserted over the hall. Two late thirteenth-century two-light windows with shouldered or 'Caernarvon' arches lit this new room from the north, and the adjacent moulded stone arch supported a staircase leading up to the newly raised parapet level. The roof trusses sat on the line of corbels, the corner one of which is carved with a bearded head. The great tower was given greater presence when four springalds, or crossbows, were winched up and placed on the four corners of the building in 1299. Indeed, in its final form the great tower was a massive building standing up to 75 feet (23m) high and — despite the extensive new buildings laid out in the lower bailey in the late thirteenth century — it remained the ceremonial focus of the castle.

A reconstruction of the Marshal brothers' great tower in the mid-thirteenth century. The division of the first-floor chamber into two rooms created a more conventional arrangement with a great hall and withdrawing room beyond. The insertion of another floor at the west end of the building created a bedchamber (Illustration by Terry Ball, 2002; with amendments 2006).

The gallery runs alongside the great tower and effectively separates the upper and middle baileys, dividing them into self-contained compartments. The row of now partly blocked arches probably served as vantage points to observe and control shipping on the river.

Right: The circular stone cistern at the bottom of the cliff below the gallery, which seems to have provided the original water supply for the castle.

Below: Marshal's Tower, the well-appointed two-storey tower at the west end of the upper bailey, was built in the very early thirteenth century, probably as a private apartment for William Marshal and his wife, Isabel.

The Gallery

The gallery is a single-storey building, which formed a roofed passage between the middle and upper baileys. It had an arcade with weakly pointed openings overlooking the river and a castellated platform above. There was a barred door to the east and — according to earlier authors — a gateway at the west end to control access through the castle and into the great tower. During the Norman and Marshal occupation of the great tower, a wooden staircase had given access to the doors at first- and second-floor level but was rendered obsolete when the gallery was built.

At the base of the cliff below the gallery is a circular stone cistern built up from the mud of the riverbank, apparently to trap water running from a natural spring in the cliff. This seems to have provided the castle's original water supply and would have been tapped using buckets operated by a winch standing just above the north-west corner of the great tower. From here, there is a good view over the cliff towards the range of buildings in the lower bailey and you can see how cleverly Ralph Gogun, the master mason, utilized the different projections and slope of the cliffs, and the cave below.

The Upper Bailey

Slight footings that extend from the back of the great tower probably represent the kitchen, bakehouse and perhaps other service buildings for the tower. The upper bailey is likely to have been the centre of William fitz Osbern's original castle; the base of the curtain wall on the landward (south) side certainly contains some early stonework dating from the Norman period. In the mid-seventeenth century, however, the curtain was reduced in height and thickened, and the sockets of decayed timber strapping can be seen halfway down the inner wall. At the same time, musketloops were inserted into this wall and that overlooking the river.

The end of the upper bailey is closed by Marshal's Tower — a two-storey rectangular tower. The first floor contains the remains of an elegant chamber lit by five finely dressed windows. Four of the windows have moulded rear arches with pointed heads and rectangular lights. The fifth, for no clear reason, has a round-headed rear arch and light. In the head of this window, there are traces of wall painting forming a pattern of red lines mimicking fine stonework. There would no doubt have been a fireplace in the missing wall as there was in the room below. The ground-floor chamber also had a drain running out over the Dell, suggesting that it was used as a kitchen. This tower belongs to the very early thirteenth century and was built by William Marshal most probably as a private apartment for himself and his wife, Isabel (pp. 10, 12). This room can be compared to the more elaborate 'domus regis' built by King John at Corfe Castle, Dorset, in the first decade of the thirteenth century.

The tower stands alongside the gateway into the upper bailey, which retains a pair of studded Tudor doors (p. 11). To the right is a latrine with a shaft

carried out over the river. Over the gateway are the remains of a staircase, which rises to the battlements of Marshal's Tower, two sides of which are pierced by arrowloops. The line of socket holes below the battlements show that the tower was equipped, in part, with a wooden hourd, or fighting platform. From the battlements, a doorway led to what was a much higher south curtain wall in the early thirteenth century, which protected the castle from the elevated ground opposite.

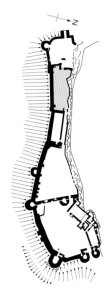

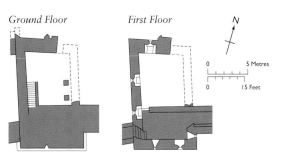

Ground Floor   *First Floor*

0   5 Metres

0   15 Feet

Below: Marshal's Tower was included in the western defences of William Marshal's castle. It contained a well-appointed private chamber over a kitchen. The wall-walk and defences were taken over the gateway and the tower, which was crowned by a wooden hourd, or fighting platform (Illustration by Chris Jones-Jenkins, 2006).

Marshal's Tower and a simple gateway overlook a deep rock-cut ditch; these formed the western defences of William Marshal's castle before the upper barbican was built.

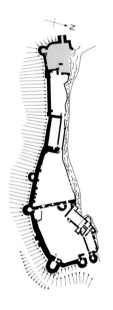

The south-west tower in the upper barbican was of a sophisticated design, equipped with an impressive battery of arrowloops to provide a wide field of fire for archers defending this vulnerable corner of the castle.

The Upper Barbican

Beyond the upper bailey gateway is a small defended platform in front of a modern bridge, which crosses a deep, rock-cut ditch to the upper barbican. This ditch marks the western limit of the castle under both the Normans and William Marshal. The heavily defended upper barbican was created in the second quarter of the thirteenth century, most probably by William Marshal's son, Gilbert, when the defensive line was extended further along the promontory to the west.

The curtain wall runs from Marshal's Tower in the upper bailey across the ditch to the south-west tower. A narrow round-headed doorway, or sallyport — which allowed defenders to leave and enter the castle almost unnoticed — in the bottom of the ditch is now blocked.

The south-west tower at the corner of the upper barbican was of a very sophisticated design to provide a wide and comprehensive field of fire for the archers at this vulnerable point in the defences. It consists of three storeys — connected by a stone spiral staircase — over an unlit basement, with the remains of a battlemented walkway around the top. Each of the upper floors was equipped with an impressive battery of arrowloops, some of which have been recently restored in red sandstone. During the seventeenth century, the tower was filled with earth, dug from within the upper barbican, and the battlements remodelled with gunports for cannon to protect the castle from artillery firing from the hill opposite.

From the south-west tower, the curtain wall curves around to the upper gatehouse. There is a line of arrowloops at what was ground level and a wall-walk, equipped with more arrowloops, protected by parapet walls inside and out. Notice how the rear parapet (parados) is built out from the wall-walk and supported on a line of corbels.

The upper gatehouse is of two phases. When first built by the sons of William Marshal, it consisted of a simple gateway through the curtain wall, similar to that in the upper bailey. Inside the gate-passage, the straight joint on the outside line of the curtain wall marks the extent of the Marshals' work; beyond, Roger Bigod added a new gatehouse, which included two murder holes, a portcullis and a drawbridge, which was made 'anew' in 1298–99.

Access to the upper rooms in the gatehouse — including the first-floor chamber from where the portcullis was operated — was via the spiral staircase in the south-west tower and along the curtain wall. From this gatehouse, there was access to the castle's gardens and the Barton, or home farm.

The curtain wall continues to cut off the end of the promontory and returns for a short length to deter any attackers from clambering around the cliff into the castle. The base of a latrine has recently been revealed at the end of this wall.

You can leave the upper barbican by the upper bailey gate or via Marshal's Tower and the curtain wall, through a breach made into the upper chamber during the seventeenth century. From here, you can either descend directly into the upper bailey, or walk along the curtain wall towards the great tower, where there is a good view of the forbidding south elevation and the Dell, a natural defence for the landward side of the castle.

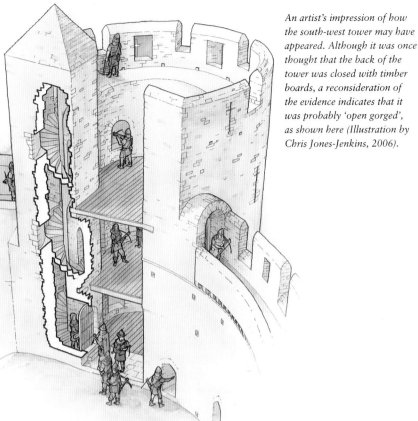

An artist's impression of how the south-west tower may have appeared. Although it was once thought that the back of the tower was closed with timber boards, a reconsideration of the evidence indicates that it was probably 'open gorged', as shown here (Illustration by Chris Jones-Jenkins, 2006).

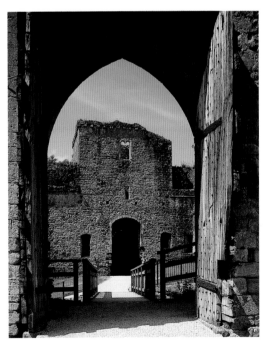

The upper gatehouse at the west end of the upper barbican was begun by the sons of William Marshal as a simple gateway and remodelled by Roger Bigod to include murder holes, a portcullis and a sophisticated drawbridge.

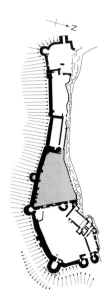

The back of the middle bailey gateway and the adjacent D-shaped tower.

The Middle Bailey

The walls and towers of the middle bailey were added to the castle by William Marshal in the late twelfth century as part of his complete remodelling of the castle's defences. However, the break in slope near the centre of this bailey may mark the position of the western defences of the Norman castle.

The entrance to the middle bailey is through a simple pointed gateway in the curtain wall, similar in design to that in the upper bailey and also containing a pair of Tudor doors. Two door jambs in the curtain wall on the cliff (north) side of the gateway suggest that there may have been a porter's lodge at this point.

This gateway was protected by a three-storey D-shaped tower projecting forward from the curtain wall. Although an original arrowloop may be seen at the rear, the ground floor of the tower was much altered when it was converted into a Tudor kitchen with the insertion of a large fireplace and a domed bread oven. The upper storeys, however, retain evidence of arrowloops and were originally reached from the wall-walk via a spiral stair, there being no access from ground level.

A low curtain wall links this tower to another of very similar design at the outer angle of the middle bailey, but it was significantly modified with the insertion of fireplaces and doorways, when the earl of Worcester developed his private ranges of rooms on either side, during the early sixteenth century (pp. 19–20). Two original, but now blocked, ground-level arrowloops and their embrasures firing over the lower bailey can still be traced (best viewed from the lower bailey).

The round corner tower would have been three storeys high when first constructed, with tiers of arrowloops commanding the Dell and the interior of the castle. It has been much altered. In the Tudor period, a door was cut through an original arrowloop and a domed roof and latrine were inserted into the ground floor (visible from the lower bailey). New windows and fireplaces turned the upper storeys into elegant chambers. Then, in the seventeenth century, when the south curtain wall was thickened and buttressed, the upper floors of the tower were modified again, to house cannon The curtain wall returns from the corner tower to a D-shaped tower — also modified during the Civil War. The thickening of the curtain wall has also hidden a sallyport at the bottom of the ditch that ran across the face of the great tower.

The middle bailey does not seem to have contained any buildings in the Middle Ages, perhaps because they would have reduced the grandeur of the approach to the main entrance of the great tower.

Before leaving the middle bailey, you may wish to explore the wall-walk and the D-shaped tower. The round towers are best inspected from the lower bailey.

The Lower Bailey

This is the most complicated part of the castle, with buildings of many different periods represented. The earliest are the twin-towered main gatehouse (pp. 10–11, 49) and the middle bailey curtain wall with its two round towers built by William Marshal at the end of the twelfth century. Any domestic accommodation that the Marshals built here, such as another hall, chambers, service rooms or stables, has been lost. The great range of buildings running along the riverside and the giant Marten's Tower were erected by Roger Bigod in the last quarter of the thirteenth century. There is considerable evidence for Tudor modifications to these buildings in the form of fireplaces in the middle bailey curtain wall, and windows in the towers of the middle bailey and Marten's Tower.

The later seventeenth-century works are represented by the massive inner curtain wall to the west (right) of Marten's Tower. This was built as part of an earth-filled sandwich between inner and outer masonry walls. The segmental-headed opening within it is the back of a stone-vaulted gunport that would have commanded the lower half of the town. The outer curtain wall has rotated outwards and split the vaulting, forcing the removal of part of the line of musketloops. Nearby is a plaque commemorating the death of Sir Nicholas Kemeys, killed after the parliamentarians captured the castle in 1648. This is probably where the curtain wall was breached during the siege.

More modern buildings — shown on old engravings as long ranges of timber-framed buildings — have been reduced to rectangular platforms in the grass.

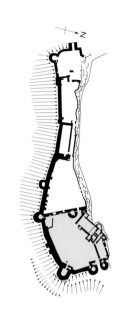

Left: The lower bailey was added to the castle by William Marshal in the late twelfth century, and substantially remodelled by Roger Bigod a hundred years later with the construction of a large domestic range and Marten's Tower. This view is looking north-east towards Roger Bigod's domestic block and the back of William Marshal's main gatehouse.

Below: The seventeenth-century gunport built into the south curtain wall of the lower bailey.

Building Stones at Chepstow Castle

Building work dating from the Norman period is characterized in particular by the use of large blocks of yellow Triassic sandstone, seen here in the east elevation of the great tower.

Over the long history of Chepstow, masons have selected a wide variety of stone to use in the construction of the castle. This choice was determined by the availability, the workability, the cost and the desirability of different sources of stone, and their identification can be very helpful in unravelling different phases of construction.

In the Norman period, large blocks of yellow Triassic sandstone were used for dressed stonework in the great tower. This stone is exposed in the cliffs at Sudbrook, 5 miles (8km) south of the castle, and can also be found as massive blocks in the ruins of the *forum-basilica* in the Roman town of *Venta Silurum* — modern-day Caerwent. Other types of stone used for facing the great tower include a wide variety of local Devonian sandstones and Carboniferous limestones, though none occur in any great quantity in the great Roman remains in the region.

One of the windows in Marshal's Tower, which is finely dressed with Dundry limestone. This distinctive creamy yellow limestone is found most often in the Marshal period works, together with grey Carboniferous limestone, which was used for rubble walling.

The Marshal period is characterized by the use of grey Carboniferous limestone — on which the castle stands — for rubble walling stone. Large blocks of creamy yellow limestone were used for the dressings. Most of this limestone comes from Dundry, near Bristol, though some in the main gatehouse is from the Bath area. Increasingly in this period, however, a reddish purple sandstone is mixed with Dundry limestone in the main openings. Some exotic stones — including dark grey Purbeck marble, polished Blue Lias and pink alabaster — were used as decoration in the great tower.

A variety of building stone was used during the Bigod period. The dressed stones of this arrowloop in Marten's Tower are made from reddish green Devonian sandstone and oolitic limestone.

Documentary accounts from the Bigod period indicate that at least some of the reddish green Devonian sandstone, used for dressed stone at this time, came from the abbey quarry just west of Tintern. The pinkish Carboniferous limestone rubble — best seen in Marten's Tower — came from across the river at Tidenham, and 'sparstone', to make plaster, was brought from Austcliff across the Severn Estuary. Wherever possible, stone was moved even short distances by boat to save cost and for ease of handling. Some oolitic limestone was used for dressings and all three types of stone are best seen in Bigod's domestic buildings in the lower bailey.

The Domestic Range

This part of the tour will guide you through the lower bailey as built by Roger Bigod, who developed a suite of apartments and lodgings appropriate for one of the richest magnates of King Edward I's reign. The domestic range consisted of two adjoining blocks linked by a central service passage, built to take advantage of the changes in height across the site. The ceremonial and private chambers of the earl occupied the higher ground to the west, and the service rooms, kitchen and additional accommodation were constructed below and on the ground sloping towards the main entrance to the castle (pp. 43–45).

Hall

Earl Roger's hall is approached via steps and a modern platform into the porch. The platform stands over a stone-lined pit, which was originally about 4 feet (1.3m) deep and seems to have been for the counterweight of a drawbridge or some other mechanism designed to give an impression that this great range of buildings could be defended or isolated from the rest of the castle.

Inside the porch, the fine vaulted ceiling springs from delicately scalloped corbels and above the main door

are two shields, painted in 1292, to look as though they hang from hooks on the wall above. The one to the right — with a single red chevron — may represent the arms of the Clare family, but that to the left — with the red ground — is too damaged to identify.

The hall, which is entered through modern doors, was paved with decorated tiles. Parts of two windows overlooking the courtyard survive, and, although damaged when the hall was converted into a glass-blowers' workshop in the 1760s, they retain the vestiges of some very finely carved floral motifs. A window overlooked the river.

At the far (west) end of the hall, there was originally a raised platform, or dais, where the high table would have been set for Roger Bigod, his family, chaplain and guests when in residence. To the left of the dais is a small square chamber, where those at the high table could withdraw from the hurly-burly of the hall — where meals could last for a long time. During the Tudor period, it was from here that stairs could be accessed leading to the earl of Worcester's new range of lodgings (pp. 19–20). The room above may have been an oratory or tiny private chapel.

Sat at the high table — laid with a white linen cloth and vessels of gold and silver — Earl Roger would have looked at the three arched doorways at

Top: The fine vaulted ceiling of the great hall porch. Traces of the painted decoration, in the form of two shields, can still be detected above the doorway into the hall.

Above: A suggested reconstruction of the painted shields and doorway from the porch into the great hall (Illustration by Bevis Sale, 2001).

Left: Roger Bigod's great hall, looking towards the service rooms that were accessed by the three ground-floor doorways. The raised doorway to the left led to the earl's chamber, or gloriette.

The remains of one of the finely carved window mouldings in Roger Bigod's great hall.

Earl's Chamber/Gloriette

Hall, Buttery and Pantry

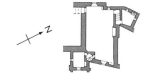

Cellar and Service Passage

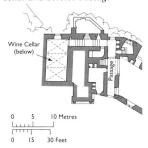

the opposite end of the hall: the left-hand door to the buttery, the larger central doorway to a flight of stairs down to the kitchen, and the right-hand doorway into the pantry. Through these doorways, food and drink for great feasts would have been brought in procession, carried by men wearing Bigod's brightly coloured livery, and led by his steward carrying his staff of office. Lesser members of the household would have sat on benches at trestle tables ranged along the sides of the room with an open hearth in the centre.

Above the central doorway is an elegant traceried window, which was probably filled with heraldic stained glass that would have cast a pool of coloured light into the hall. To the left of the window, at a slightly lower level, there is another door which led to the earl's chamber, or gloriette, (pp. 16, 42) and must have been approached by a wooden staircase.

Earl's Chamber

Today, however, visitors approach the earl's chamber via one of the service rooms — the buttery — through the left-hand door. Here, the butler would have put wine and beer in flagons and jugs to be taken into the hall. Note how an ingenious drain was contrived into the wall over the cliff.

A modern stairway leads to the earl's chamber, originally perhaps the most lavishly decorated room in the complex. This room would have been a combination of a bedchamber, a private sitting room — where some meals may have been taken — and an audience chamber, where the most important guests would have been entertained and the earl's more private business carried out. The exhibition — which includes the original doors from the main gatehouse (p. 11) — now occupies what must have been an impressive space with windows overlooking the gorge of the river Wye and the courtyard of the castle. A doorway leads to a well-appointed latrine carried out over the river. There is a large and elaborate fireplace and a low-pitched roof would have been carried on the distinctive corbel table.

To earn the name, gloriette, this chamber must have been very special or exotic. The walls may have displayed an elaborate scheme of narrative paintings, been studded with semi-precious stones or hung with Italian silk. The gloriette at Hesdin (Pas de Calais), belonging to Count Robert of Artois, even had a fake tree with gilded birds that spouted

A reconstruction of Roger Bigod's domestic range about 1300. The buildings are seen from the riverward side of the castle: the great hall is to the right, with the cellar below; in the centre are the service rooms with the earl's chamber above and to the left are the kitchen and apartments (Illustration by Terry Ball, 2002).

Right: The exquisitely decorated lodge, La Zisa, in Palermo, Sicily, built on the Arab model of the glorietta or ziza (John Goodall).

Gloriettes

Roger Bigod's building accounts make several mentions of 'La Gloriette'. Repaired in 1271, it implies that there was already a building of this name erected by an earlier lord of Chepstow, perhaps even William Marshal himself. Later references specifically link the 'Gloriette' to Earl Roger's new chamber at the centre of the domestic range in the lower bailey.

The word, 'gloriette', seems to have been derived from the Spanish, '*glorieta*', now most commonly meaning a pavilion set in the centre of a formal garden. An alternative derivation from the Romance languages could mean 'glorious' or 'magnificent', and in Arabic the equivalent word is '*aziz*'. Buildings of this type are found at Moorish palaces in Spain, where more elaborate lodges were set out in the adjacent parks. At Granada, the Generalife, an arcaded building set around pools and fountains, was the *glorietta* or '*ziza*' of the Alhambra Palace. The Norman kings of Sicily were the first Europeans

to adopt the Arab model, and an exquisitely decorated lodge, La Zisa, survives from the royal park in Palermo.

Edward I's wife, Eleanor of Castile, is often credited with introducing the gloriette into England. At Leeds Castle, Kent, part of the queen's estate, a finely decorated private apartment was created for the king on an island in the moat, connected to the castle by a covered bridge. Gloriettes seem to have had two main requirements: privacy for the lord or his lady away from the main business of the castle, and a location making the most of the natural beauty of the surroundings. There are earlier buildings of this type in England. King John built what was later called a gloriette in the inner bailey of Corfe Castle, Dorset, soon after 1200, separated from the other buildings by a gatehouse and covered bridge. In the 1170s, King Henry II made a walled bower for his mistress, Rosamund Clifford, at Everswell, Oxfordshire, containing gardens and pools on the Arab model.

Chepstow's late thirteenth-century gloriette centred around the earl's chamber. Bigod may have swept away the earlier structure of this name when creating his domestic range in the lower bailey, though it is possible that Marshal's Tower in the upper bailey was an earlier gloriette. His chamber could be isolated from the adjacent rooms, and the playful defensive form of the hall porch is reminiscent of Corfe. Its cliff-top location was chosen to get the most spectacular view of the river gorge. It was this view which, in reverse, was to provide the climax of the Wye valley tour for the travellers of the eighteenth and nineteenth centuries seeking the Picturesque experience.

Leeds Castle, Kent, where a finely decorated apartment, described as a gloriette, was created on an island in the moat for King Edward I. The location perhaps emphasizes the requirements of a gloriette — isolation and beautiful natural surroundings (Jeremy Ashbee).

water on his surprised guests. These special rooms allowed their owners to live like heroes of the medieval romances and take the greatest delight in their wealth and sophistication.

Return to the great hall via the stone spiral staircase and the pantry below. At the head of these stairs is a small heated chamber over the porch (not now accessible), which may have been a closet or the most private room for the earl or his countess. Leave the hall through the central doorway, down the flight of steps into the service passage.

Service Passage

The service passage divides the domestic range into two main parts, separating the kitchen and domestic apartments from the earl's ceremonial and private rooms, which were described above. Originally, the passage was two storeys high and had a stout, barred door to seal off this area from the courtyard. The large arched opening opposite the foot of the stairs contains the remains of three service hatches, through which dishes would have been passed from the kitchen to liveried servants to take up to the hall. The small room opposite the hatch probably served as the office for the administration of supplies to the castle. To the left of the hatch, towards the river, is a door to a set of latrines, corbelled out rather perilously over the river. Just beyond is a pair of cupboards, rebated for wooden doors.

The passage turns left and begins to descend a long flight of stairs. Immediately on the left is a windowless room, perhaps a wine cellar, from where jugs of wine could be taken to the buttery. Even though the earl and his household would not have spent much of the year at Chepstow, consumption of wine could be enormous. For example, when Edward II's brothers, Thomas and Edmund, and their retinues stayed at Chepstow for three and a half months in 1311–12, they consumed five barrels and a pipe of wine worth £25.

Down the first flight of stairs is a landing, given architectural emphasis by a vaulted ceiling, with steps up to a door leading outside. Here, the cliffs form a natural balcony framed by the two great buttresses supporting the gloriette above. The walls surrounding the balcony are Tudor in date and in the thirteenth century the platform may have been open or enclosed with just a fence. The architectural emphasis given by the vaulting suggests that this

was perhaps a place for the lord and not his household servants. Like the gloriette, it hints at a fascination with the beauty of the landscape of the lower Wye valley and the rocky surface may originally have supported a small garden. It is also the best place to see how the cellar was built over the cave below by using a succession of arches to support the masonry above.

Cellar

Return to the stairs and descend into the cellar, which lies beneath the lower end of the hall. This is a splendid room consisting of three bays of quadripartite rib vaulting sprung from corbels carved with fine detail. The cellar was used to store barrels of wine and ale. There is no brewhouse in the castle because the earl was entitled to one-eighth of all the ale brewed in Chepstow for use in his household. This was collected in 32-gallon barrels that could be winched up by a stout pulley arm projecting out of the doorway over the river, lashed to a giant iron ring set into the floor. Boats could beach within the cave below and their cargo could be lifted directly into the cellar.

Above: The stairs leading from the service passage to the cellar. At the foot of the first flight, a door leads to a natural balcony above the river Wye.

Below: The cellar, roofed with fine quadripartite vaults, provided storage for beer and wine. Barrels could be winched up to the cellar directly from boats beached below.

Above: The area occupied by the kitchen lies in the foreground, to the west of the modern shop. The shop is built on the site of the medieval larder and there were two chambers above.

Servants preparing food for diners in the great hall are shown in this detail from the fourteenth-century Luttrell Psalter *(British Library, Additional Ms. 42130, f. 207v).*

Kitchen

Return up the stairs and along the service passage to the kitchen. Like the cellar, the kitchen was built on a vast scale to provide food for the huge feasts held in the hall, and was given bold architectural expression to reflect the importance of hospitality in the life of the castle. The building accounts show that work had begun on the kitchen in 1282, and it must have been in use by the time of the visit of King Edward I and Queen Eleanor in December 1284. Nevertheless, work must have continued as late as 1291 when the accounts record the sawing and planing of planks to make a great 'board', or table, for this kitchen.

The room is not square and was open right through to a lead roof. The corbels and sockets for the ends of the roof trusses can be seen on both side walls. The kitchen was lit by three large, unglazed, mullioned and transomed windows (two survive), set quite high in the walls so that light fell onto the working areas. Cooking must have been done both in a large oven in the corner of the room — the base of which survives abutting the shop — and on a series of open hearths with the smoke and fumes being drawn out through an elaborate louvre in the centre of the roof. This louvre survived to be drawn in the mid-nineteenth century and was described as being partly made of glazed pottery. Tables for preparing and plating up the food would have been ranged around the walls before the dishes were passed through the serving hatch.

The remains of an elaborate drain or waste disposal system can be seen in the floor near the door to the shop. The massive chimney and the base of the oven on the cliff side are Tudor alterations. Also on this side is a doorway opening out onto the cliff edge. The roof line on the outside wall shows that this provided a covered area where goods could be hauled up into the kitchen from the river, similar to the arrangements made for the cellar, and so avoiding carting the meat, flour, salt and other bulky goods through the main gatehouse.

Between the kitchen and the gatehouse — in the space now occupied by the castle shop — was the larder. There were two chambers above and all three rooms were provided with a private latrine.

Exterior of the Domestic Range

Leave the domestic range via the service passage and enter the courtyard of the lower bailey. Looking back towards the kitchen, you will see a blocked doorway into the earl's chamber above the entrance to the main service passage. To the right there are doorways that led into the middle and upper chambers over the larder. Between these doorways is a line of stone corbels and a second, corresponding row survives below the battlemented parapet. These corbels indicate that there was a three-storey, timber-framed pentice, or lean-to, built against the face of the building. It not only provided a covered passage at the rear of the gatehouse but also contained a staircase up to the chambers alongside the kitchen. From there a platform ran in front of the kitchen window and up another staircase into the earl's chamber. This allowed the earl's principal servants — perhaps his chamberlain, steward and chaplain — direct and sheltered access from their chambers into the earl's chamber, without the need to descend to ground level or go through the kitchen itself.

Left: An early nineteenth-century drawing by John Buckler of the louvre that once allowed smoke and fumes to escape from the centre of the kitchen roof (British Library, Additional Ms. 36371, f. 67v).

Below: Roger Bigod's later thirteenth-century domestic block, which was cleverly modelled by his master mason, Ralph Gogun, to take advantage of the changes in ground level. Entrance was by way of a porch, which was decorated with painted shields.

Opposite: Marten's Tower has been described as 'a mural tower to end all mural towers'. Supported on spurred buttresses and crowned with carved figures, this massive tower dominates the southern defences of the castle. Inside, the plastered walls of the comfortable apartments (left) were decorated with red and yellow ochre wall paintings, enough of which survive to allow the decorative scheme to be reconstructed (below left) (Illustration by Bevis Sale, 2001).

Marten's Tower

Marten's Tower, or the 'New Tower' as it was referred to in Roger Bigod's accounts, was begun around 1288 and brought into use by 1293. It was begun after the earl's domestic apartments had been completed and almost certainly replaced an earlier tower dating from the Marshal period. Marten's Tower has been described as 'a mural tower to end all mural towers', but it is far more than a simple defensive work. In addition to the three storeys visible from the courtyard, there is a basement, a room in the roof space and a private chapel carried out over the curtain wall to the left (east). The castle well is just alongside the door.

As you enter the tower, note the slot for a portcullis, which protected the entrance and was operated from the window reveal above. Note also the Tudor door, which has three loops for pistols cut in it. Above the unlit basement, the ground floor was equipped with three arrowloops, but they do not provide a comprehensive field of fire compared with that in the south-west tower of the upper barbican (pp. 13, 34–35). Built after King Edward I's successful conquest of Wales (1282–83), this is more an exercise in geometry than defence.

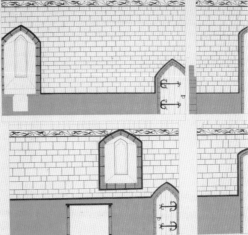

Both the first- and second-floor chambers were quite well lit, with narrow windows looking across the town and larger windows — replaced in the Tudor period — overlooking the courtyard. Each floor has a fireplace — the smaller one at first-floor level is another Tudor alteration — and access to a private latrine. The walls were plastered and enough survives of the red and yellow ochre paintwork to reconstruct their original decoration, which according to the building accounts was painted in 1292. Timber

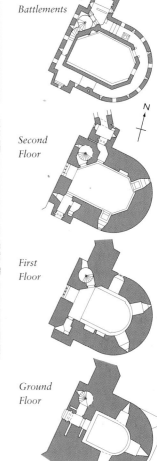

Battlements

Chapel

Second Floor

First Floor

Ground Floor

| 0 | 5 | 10 Metres |
| 0 | 15 | 30 Feet |

Right: The small, but beautifully decorated, private chapel in Marten's Tower.

One of the five carved figures on the battlements of Marten's Tower. The figures include a soldier bearing a shield, a musician and a knight.

Like Marten's Tower, the Eagle Tower at Caernarfon Castle, built by King Edward I in the late thirteenth century, also contained a suite of comfortable apartments and was decorated with carved figures on the battlements.

floors and ceilings would have been carried on the corbel tables running around the tower. The far end of the second-floor chamber is hexagonal rather than semicircular in plan and the two lancet windows are provided with seats. From this level, there was access onto curtain wall-walks to the north and south, each protected by a door and a portcullis operated from above.

Continue up the spiral staircase and you reach a small but beautiful private chapel. All the tracery of the east window has been lost but the jambs are carved with rosettes and the traces of two eagles can be seen partway up each jamb. On each side of the chapel is a lancet window with a semicircular-backed seat contrived in the sill. A tiny aumbry, or cupboard, where the communion vessels were stored, survives in the south wall. Rather inconveniently, there is also a slot in the floor for a portcullis, which would have blocked the altar when raised. The portcullis, however, must have been light enough to have been raised by hand as there is no space for a winch.

Continue up to the battlemented wall-walk, part of which was roofed to provide cover for the portcullis above the south door to the tower from the curtain wall below. Another room with a

fireplace was contrived within the roof space. The most remarkable feature is the line of five carved figures, each seated on a merlon pierced by an arrowloop within a Caernarvon arch. These figures look out to greet those approaching the castle and include a soldier with a shield, a musician with a viol, a scholar with a scroll, and a cross-legged knight.

But why did Roger Bigod build this remarkable new tower, equipped with its own suite of lodgings and private chapel, when he had already provided a complete complex of apartments for himself and his household on the opposite side of the lower bailey? This was a suite possibly intended for important guests, the most significant of whom would have been King Edward I and his consort. Construction began after the king's visit in 1284 and although it was habitable before the earl's confrontation with Edward in 1297 (pp. 14–17), it may never have been used for its intended purpose. Structures with a similar purpose seem to have been built elsewhere in the Marches, including the south tower at Stokesay Castle, and Acton Burnell Castle, in Shropshire. In Wales, there is the inner east gatehouse at Caerphilly Castle, and the king himself built the Eagle Tower at Caernarfon Castle with battlements adorned with human heads and standing eagles. By adopting a military form the 'New Tower' not only contributed to the defensive circuit of the castle but also symbolized Edward I's military success. The portcullises allowed the tower — and its occupants — to be isolated from the rest of the business of the castle; and the figures on the battlements perhaps represented different attributes of the king's personality. This tower was intended to flatter and impress, and, like those built elsewhere in the March, was a requirement for everyone in the king's inner circle.

The new tower was later made into fine Tudor apartments that survived to serve as Henry Marten's well-appointed prison between 1668 and 1680 (pp. 23–24). It remained roofed and floored into the nineteenth century, which explains why the interiors are so well preserved. The gable wall at roof level of the tower did not fall until about 1900.

You can return to the lower bailey through Marten's Tower or via the wall-walk at second-floor level, which leads to a spiral staircase in the main gatehouse. From here you can see the succession of chambers that make up the interior of the gatehouse.

The front façade of the twin-towered gatehouse, built to a revolutionary design by William Marshal in the 1190s and subsequently modified by Roger Bigod in the late thirteenth century. Further alterations, including the square-headed windows in the round towers, were made in the sixteenth century, and the battlements were remodelled after the Civil War.

Battlements

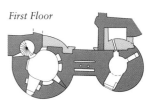

Second Floor

First Floor

Ground Floor

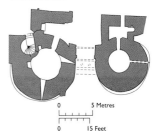

The Main Gatehouse

Apparently built by William Marshal almost immediately after his marriage to Isabel of Clare in 1189, the gatehouse is of a revolutionary design (p. 10). It consists of two round towers of slightly different diameter built close together and well equipped with arrowloops to provide a wide field of fire. Between the towers the gate-passage was protected — from front to back — by murder holes, a portcullis with counterweights passing down through neatly constructed circular shafts, a pair of iron-clad doors (now in the exhibition) and a second portcullis. Outside, there was a small barbican, which further protected the entrance.

Roger Bigod added square chambers to the rear of the round towers, which extended the gate-passage. The round tower to the left (north) was the castle's prison (accessible from the shop) and that to the right was a guardroom. Across the back of the gate towers, a large rectangular chamber — whose blocked fireplace can still be seen — occupied the second floor and connected to other rooms in the towers. These chambers were probably the apartments of the constable, who managed the castle when his lord was away.

The battlements, which were later modified to mount cannon, provided a fighting platform to protect the gateway from any attackers. This is thought to be the oldest twin-towered gatehouse in Britain and demonstrates that William Marshal and his master craftsmen were at the forefront of castle design, building on their experiences in France and the Holy Land.

In the Middle Ages the principal approach to the castle was from the east, where, apart from a large pond, there were no natural obstacles to an attack. Not only would the main gatehouse and Marten's Tower have impressed visitors — as they still do today — but they would also have served as formidable defences against any assault on this vulnerable side of the castle.

The Exterior of the Castle

This section provides a short tour around the exterior of the castle, along part of the Port, or town, Wall to the town's gatehouse, back through the historic market square, with an option to visit the priory church before returning to the castle car park, a distance of about one mile (1.5 km).

On leaving the castle, note the slots for portcullises, doors and murder holes that protect the main entrance. The two towers of the gatehouse are slightly different, the one to the left has a taller flared base and the scar of a wall indicating the existence of a barbican providing a forward defence to the main castle doors. This seems to have terminated on the cliff edge, rather than against the right-hand tower. Four tiers of arrowloops can be traced on both towers. Just below the wall top is a line of square sockets for the wooden beams of a hourd (a fighting platform) built in front of the battlements.

Walking towards Marten's Tower, the curtain wall was raised by Roger Bigod to connect with the upper level of the gatehouse. From the outside, the

sheer scale of Marten's Tower cannot fail to impress. It is D-shaped in plan with spur buttresses, which were very fashionable in the late thirteenth century. The arrowloop to the front has been modified with a circular gunloop. The stringcourse below the castellations has two lion's masks acting as drains from the wall-walk. The statues ringing the top of the tower can be seen high above.

Walking up the Dell, it is possible to identify several building phases in the curtain wall of the lower bailey (between Marten's Tower and the corner round tower of the middle bailey). This is the area where the breach is likely to have been made during the Civil War siege. The outer framework of the great gunport can be seen; so too can some of the musketloops that ran along the top of this wall. Both ends of this section of the curtain wall and the two buttresses were built about a hundred years ago.

Continuing up the Dell, the curtain wall, corner and D-shaped towers of William Marshal's middle bailey can be seen. Some of the early thirteenth-century arrowloops and the battlements have been modified by seventeenth-century alterations. Low down is the blocked round arch of a sallyport. The south elevation of the great tower is its most forbidding aspect. The massive blocks of the plinth and the band of Roman tiles run downslope, and the

The arrowloop on the front of Marten's Tower that was later modified with a gunloop.

The southern defences of the castle overlooking the Dell on the landward side of the castle. The south-west tower of the upper barbican is in the foreground.

wall is divided into five bays by pilasters. The only significant alteration from the Norman period is the early thirteenth-century window inserted through one of the buttresses. The upper storey, built in two phases in the thirteenth century, was perhaps destroyed by gunfire in the Civil War.

The curtain wall of the upper bailey contains some large blocks of stone near its base, evidence for the curtain wall of the Norman castle. The curtain wall built by William Marshal was originally up to 14 feet (4.5m) higher, but was reduced in the seventeenth century when the musketloops were created. It stood almost as high as Marshal's Tower, the rectangular tower that formed the south-west corner of William Marshal's castle (pp. 12, 32–33). The upper barbican was added a generation later and is dominated by the south-west tower, one of the finest defensive towers to be found anywhere. The restored arrowloops show how narrow they were originally. There is also another sallyport, on the line of the upper bailey ditch. You may wish to walk around to the gatehouse and see the modifications undertaken in the late thirteenth century.

The Port Wall

Continue up the Dell and climb up steps cut into the grassy bank to your left and you will reach the town wall — the Port Wall. This wall cuts off a loop in the river Wye to protect the town and port of Chepstow. There is no documentary evidence for when it was built, though it is likely to date from the lordship of Roger Bigod (p. 14). Originally it extended for 1,200 yards (1,100m), with ten D-shaped towers, and enclosed an area

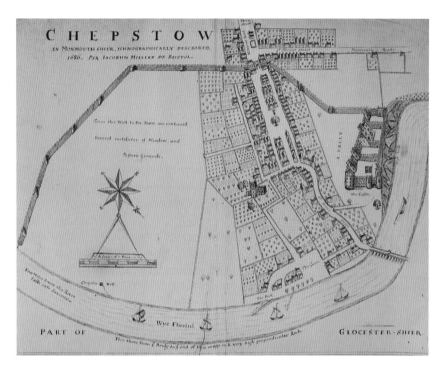

Jacob Millerd's map of Chepstow, dated 1686, shows the castle, the town and the full extent of the town walls, set in a loop in the river Wye (Newport Borough Libraries).

The town gate was originally the only gate in the Port Wall. Built by Roger Bigod in the thirteenth century, it was much rebuilt and altered in the Tudor period. The windows, battlements and internal arches are nineteenth- and twentieth-century additions.

of 130 acres (50ha). Early maps show that the town and castle occupied only the northern third of the walled area; the rest was taken up by gardens, orchards or meadows.

Enter the car park through a Tudor doorway inserted into the wall. If you turn left and walk to the grassy area at the far (east) end of the car park, there is a magnificent panorama of the castle. When you return, walk along the inside of the wall, passing the northern end, which is now a rectangular, open-backed tower of uncertain date. Originally, the wall ran from here across the Dell and turned to join the south-west tower of the castle. The wall has a wall-walk and parapet and is protected by D-shaped towers projecting forward, the first of which is within the car park.

Leave the car park by the vehicle entrance and follow the Port Wall to see the base of the next tower and how the wall has been incorporated into later houses. Continue to Welsh Street, turn left and walk towards the town, turn left again and look at the town gate. This was the only gate in the Port Wall, where tolls and taxes were paid on goods entering the town. Its origins may be in a D-shaped tower of the thirteenth century. In 1524, it was extended and the upper storey was made into a prison for the town by the first earl of

Worcester. His arms appear on two draped shields, now worn, on the outer face of the gate. The windows, battlements and internal archways are nineteenth- and twentieth-century restorations. Pass through the pedestrian archway on the right-hand side of the gate.

By turning right, the Port Wall can be followed for much of its length to the south, where it has been truncated by the railway, but to get a better sense of the medieval town, walk straight down the hill. You pass through the long rectangular market place, which was the focus of the town's commercial life. In the Middle Ages it would have been open and stalls would have been erected on market days and during fairs. In the 1280s, Roger Bigod built the Bothall, a small covered market hall in the centre of the town. Jacob Millerd's map, however, shows that some buildings had been built down its centre by 1686, to be succeeded by the more modern buildings of today. The main merchants' houses would have lined the market place and a fine stone-vaulted cellar survives below the British Legion. Look for new plaques set into the pavement giving the history of each shop.

Continue through the pedestrianized section of road until you reach Sir Walter Montague's Almshouses, which closed the end of the medieval market place. Begun in 1614, they are typical of the charitable foundations of the period. Turn right and you can visit St Mary's Church, which incorporates the west front and nave of the Norman Benedictine priory, founded by William fitz Osbern (p. 5). The church contains the tomb chest and effigies of Henry, second earl of Worcester (d. 1549), and his wife, Elizabeth.

Return past Sir Walter Montague's Almshouses and you reach the Thomas Powis Almshouses of 1716. Follow Bridge Street back to the car park in front of the castle, or continue and cross the magnificent cast-iron bridge. Completed in 1816 by John Urpeth Rastrick (d. 1856) — later famed as a great railway engineer — it replaced the medieval and later wooden bridge, which had had a stone gateway at its centre. Looking back towards the castle, you will have the same view as painted by Turner and other famous artists. Chepstow Museum, with its remarkable collection of paintings and engravings of the castle, is opposite the entrance to the castle car park.

Chepstow Bulwarks Camp

J. K. Knight BA, FSA

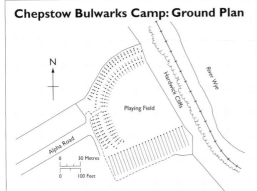

An aerial view of the small Iron Age promontory fort of Chepstow Bulwarks Camp, overlooking the river Wye (Royal Commission on the Ancient and Historical Monuments of Wales).

Take the A48 south-west from Chepstow town centre and turn left at the road signposted to Bulwark. Continue for half a mile past the shops to a small roundabout. Bear left down Bulwark Avenue and turn immediately left down Alpha Road. The camp is at the far end.

Bulwarks Camp is a small promontory fort of the pre-Roman Iron Age, overlooking the river Wye, here a tidal water, near its confluence with the Severn. On the east (river) side of the camp, Hardwick Cliffs, some 170 feet (52m) high, are a formidable defence. To the south is a natural slope. The western and northern sides, which lack natural defence, are protected by a substantial bivallate (double) earthen rampart, with a main inner bank and a lesser outer bank. The inner bank has hints of a drystone revetment on its outer face, visible where the bank is eroded. The area enclosed within the camp defences is somewhat less than 2.5 acres (1ha).

The site has never been explored by archaeological excavation, and nothing is known of its history. It is, however, one of a series of hillforts and defended enclosures in south-east Wales built by the late Iron Age tribe of the Silures, who gave the legions so much trouble in the period AD 50–75. The hillforts, with their often massive banked and ditched earthwork defences, are probably some centuries older than this.

They may well represent the defended seats of tribal notables or chieftains, perhaps akin to the *equites* or knights whom Julius Caesar recorded as playing a leading role in the somewhat similar tribal society of Gaul. These pre-Roman forts tend to fall into two broad groups: the smaller examples as here at Chepstow, and the much larger sites — the true hillforts — with greater enclosed areas and more massive defences. It would, however, be difficult to say whether this division represents some form of ranking or social stratification among tribal lords.

Whatever their ranking, we know from excavation of similar sites that these forts represent communities of people living in circular timber houses and practising a mixed agricultural economy — growing wheat and barley (the latter for brewing as well as for bread) and keeping cattle and other domestic livestock. Their economy supported craftsmen (and women) such as potters, weavers and blacksmiths. The inhabitants also traded further afield for some necessities such as containers of salt which could not be obtained locally.

Today, the ramparts at Bulwarks Camp are wooded and much overgrown, whilst the interior of the site is leased to the local authority for use as a play area. Two larger hillforts can be visited nearby at Llanmelin (in the care of Cadw) above Caerwent, and at Sudbrook Camp near Portskewett.

Runston Church

J. K. Knight BA, FSA

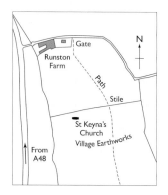

Right: Runston Church from the south-west. At one stage there was a tower at the west end, later replaced by a bellcote which survives to gable height.

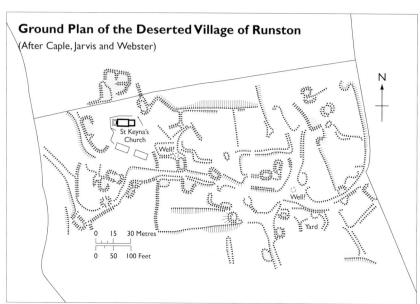

Ground Plan of the Deserted Village of Runston
(After Caple, Jarvis and Webster)

The Medieval Background

The site of the deserted village of Runston stands on a low hill or plateau of oolitic limestone some 3 miles (4.8km) west of Chepstow, and just to the north of the Chepstow–Newport road (NGR ST 495916). The village was a product of the Anglo-Norman settlement of Gwent Is-Coed (Gwent 'below the wood', south of the Wentwood ridge), following the establishment of Chepstow Castle in the late eleventh century. The ruins of the twelfth-century Norman church are in the care of Cadw, and they may be reached by taking the footpath that lies to the east of Runston Farm.

There are many villages and small settlements in the southern Welsh coastal plain, whose names combine that of their original Norman owners with the suffix '-ton', meaning a farm or settlement. Hence, there is Gileston — 'Giles's farm', or Bishton — 'the bishop's

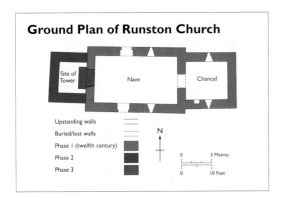

Ground Plan of Runston Church

Site of Tower · Nave · Chancel

Upstanding walls
Buried/lost walls
Phase 1 (twelfth century)
Phase 2
Phase 3

N

0 — 3 Metres
0 — 10 Feet

The chancel arch, with its good-quality ashlar jambs and rounded arch.

(of Llandaff) manor'. The latter replaced the original Welsh name, Llancadwaladr, which may have been difficult for the tongues of Anglo-Norman settlers. Runston — known in a document of 1245 as 'Runestun' and as 'Ryngeston' in another dated 1262 — was presumably the farm or settlement of someone with a name like Rhun or Runa. We do not know who he was, but he or his successor would have been responsible for building the village church, at a time when manorial lords through much of Britain were building new parish churches in stone, supported by tithes, and burial and baptismal offerings from their tenants. The dedication is to St Keyna, probably the patron of Keynsham in Somerset, and of whom the lord of Runston had perhaps obtained a relic.

A Description of the Church

The church consists of a simple rectangular nave and square chancel, and is very similar to other small Anglo-Norman churches in the area, such as nearby Portskewett. At one stage there was a square west tower, but this was later demolished and replaced by a bellcote. Only the foundations of the tower, found during conservation work, now remain. The nave and chancel stand largely intact to full gable height, and lack only the roof. They are built of locally quarried limestone: coursed rubble for the walls and squared blocks of good-quality dressed ashlar for the quoins, door and window openings, and the chancel arch. Many of the small square putlog holes, which held the wooden scaffolding used during the construction of the church, can still be seen.

The chancel was originally lit by a pair of splayed round-headed windows in the north and south walls, with a third window in the centre of the east wall, but

this has vanished during later rebuilding work. A small recess in the south wall was probably a piscina, a basin in which the sacred vessels were washed after Mass. The chancel arch remains intact: the masonry jambs, plain chamfered imposts and round-headed arch are all in good-quality ashlar. Like the chancel, the nave had a pair of round-headed windows, but only the northern one survives intact. There were doors to the north and south, both in round-headed openings, which would have been similar to the chancel arch, when complete. Each door may have had a tympanum — a stone panel, possibly decorated, filling the semicircular space between door and arch.

At the west end of the church, the foundations of the tower can be seen, built against the earliest Norman masonry and clearly later in date. At some period the tower was abandoned and a large buttress built to support a bellcote. A fourteenth-century font, now in the National Museum, Cardiff, is thought to come from the church.

The Decline and Abandonment of the Village and Church

Some twenty-five house sites, including a possible manor house complex, are visible around the church and these probably represent the expansion of the village to its maximum extent. In the later Middle Ages, the population of Britain was falling due to climatic deterioration and pestilence, and many settlements on poorer marginal land declined. Runston was no exception. By the middle of the sixteenth century, a survey suggests that there were

The deeply splayed round-arched window in the north wall of the nave.

no more than nine houses still occupied. The church remained in use for burials into the eighteenth century, the last person being laid to rest about 1770. By 1772, the number of houses had declined to six and according to two Victorian antiquaries, 'the cottages which formed the village were purposely allowed to fall to the ground, as the best way of dislodging the inhabitants who were a most lawless

The church stands near the north-western edge of the former medieval village, now represented by no more than a series of earthworks.

and troublesome set of people, subsisting by smuggling, sheep stealing, poaching and other predatory acts… '. We should, however, bear in mind that forest edge communities like Runston had a long tradition of independence of mind in matters such as firewood, rabbits, and small game, and this was not always appreciated by landlords and gamekeepers (both antiquaries were county landowners).

However exaggerated the reports of such lawlessness, it is all too likely that the landowners — the Lewis family of St Pierre and Penhow — did all they could to encourage the tenants to leave by allowing the houses to fall into ruin. Runston had in any case always been a poor and marginal village and there were new jobs nearby in the developing port of Newport, and in the new towns of industrial Monmouthshire. By the time Archdeacon William Coxe visited Runston in 1798 (in the moonlight, in the Romantic tradition), the village — including the church — had become an archaeological site.

Further Reading

Acknowledgements
The author and Cadw would like to thank John Allen, Jeremy Ashbee, Peter Brears, Nicola Coldstream, the late Rees Davies, John Goodall, Jeremy Knight, Dan Miles, Marc Morris, Stephen Priestley, David Robinson and Bevis Sale for their help in compiling this guidebook.

Chepstow Castle
Jeremy A. Ashbee, '"The Chamber called Gloriette": Living at Leisure in Thirteenth- and Fourteenth-Century Castles', *Journal of British Archaeological Association* **157** (2004), 17–40.

R. Avent, 'The Late Twelfth-Century Gatehouse at Chepstow Castle, Monmouthshire, Wales', *Château Gaillard* **20** (2002), 141–51.

D. Bates, *William the Conqueror* (London 1989); reprinted with revisions (Stroud 2001).

G. T. Clark, 'Chepstow Castle', *Transactions of the Bristol and Gloucestershire Archaeological Society* **6** (1881–82), 51–74.

D. Crouch, *William Marshal: Knighthood, War and Chivalry, 1147–1219, second edition* (London 2002).

R. R. Davies, *Conquest, Coexistence and Change: Wales 1063–1415* (Oxford 1987); reprinted in paperback as, *The Age of Conquest: Wales 1063–1415* (Oxford 1991).

P. Gaunt, *A Nation Under Siege: The Civil War in Wales 1642–48* (London 1991).

M. Morris, *The Bigod Earls of Norfolk in the Thirteenth Century* (Woodbridge, 2005).

M. Prestwich, *Edward I* (London 1988); new edition (New Haven and London 1997).

J. C. Perks, 'The Architectural History of Chepstow Castle during the Middle Ages', *Transactions of the Bristol and Gloucestershire Archaeological Society* **67** (1946–48), 307–46.

J. C. Perks, *Chepstow Castle, Monmouthshire*, second edition (HMSO, London 1967).

T. Purser, 'William Fitz Osbern, Earl of Hereford: Personality and Power on the Welsh Frontier, 1066–71', in M. Strickland (ed.), *Armies, Chivalry and Warfare in Medieval Britain and France* (Stamford 1998), 133–46.

R. C. Turner, 'The Great Tower, Chepstow Castle, Wales', *Antiquaries Journal* **84** (2004), 223–317.

R. C. Turner and A. Johnson (eds), *Chepstow Castle* (Leominster 2006).

J. G. Wood, *The Lordship, Castle & Town of Chepstow, otherwise Striguil* (Newport 1910).

Runston Chapel
R. Caple, P. H. Jarvis and P. V. Webster, 'The Deserted Village of Runston, Gwent: A Field Survey', *Bulletin of the Board of Celtic Studies* **27** (1976–78), 638–52.

O. Morgan and T. Wakeman, *Notes on the Ecclesiastical Remains at Runston, Sudbrook, Dinham and Llan-bedr* (Newport 1858).